Find the Magician!

Also by Hank Whittemore

THE MAN WHO RAN THE SUBWAYS
The Story of Mike Quill

COP!
A Close-up of Violence and Tragedy

FEELING IT
A Novel

TOGETHER
A Reporter's Journey into the
New Black Politics

THE SUPER COPS
The True Story of the Cops
Called Batman and Robin

PEROFF
The Man Who Knew too Much

Find the Magician!

The Counterfeiting Crime of the Century

HANK WHITTEMORE

THE VIKING PRESS   NEW YORK

Library of Congress Cataloging in Publication Data
Whittemore, Hank.
Find the magician!
1. Counterfeits and counterfeiting—
Great Britain.   I. Title
HG336.G7W47   364.1'33   80-5510
ISBN 0-670-31738-1

Printed in the United States of America
Set in CRT Caledonia

Find the Magician!

Prologue

In June 1975, British newspapers carried some intriguing headlines about revelations being made in England's Old Bailey, the Central Criminal Court in London:

"SPY" BUSTS FIVERS GANG

A taxi took American businessman Mark Yarry on a trip to adventure in the underworld. . . .

He helped to expose a massive forgery ring which could have caused a financial crisis—and might even have broken the Bank of England. . . .

The operation took 35-year-old Mr. Yarry to secret meetings at exclusive hotels and restaurants, with his detective colleague monitoring conversations through a radio microphone in his tie-clip.

"MAGICIAN" OF FORGED FIVERS

A man known as The Magician was a genius at producing forged fivers, it was claimed at the Old Bailey yesterday. . . .

END OF GREAT FIVERS PLOT
Phony 'Mafia' Agents
Foil Big Forgery Gang

A forgery gang who tried to break the Bank of England was smashed yesterday.

They printed fivers so perfect that only electronic sorting machines could tell if they were dud.

They fell because they were foiled by two daring men—a civilian and a policeman—posing as Mafia gangsters. . . .

1

The gang of forged note-pushers was one of the most active and successful known to Scotland Yard in modern times. . . .

Presiding over the courtroom was His Honor Judge King-Hamilton, Queen's Counsel, who remarked, "There is a world of difference between this case and hundreds and hundreds of cases that have been before the courts." The barrister leading the defense agreed, but mainly because the American, Mark Yarry, and the so-called Magician, the "genius" of a forger, were such mysterious characters. "M'Lord," the barrister shouted, "there is more to this case than meets the eye!"

And so there was. What follows is the true story of what happened during nine weeks in the fall of 1974. The events have been reconstructed from official documents, personal notes and diaries, transcripts of secret tape recordings, and direct interviews with key participants.

ACT I

Spring 1972

It was a cool, bright morning in London, just before eleven o'clock, when the forger entered the central office of one of England's oldest and largest banks. He strode across the plush, deep-blue carpet toward the tellers' windows and took his place in line. As he waited, the forger experienced the inner calm of a man who had total confidence in what he was about to do. This was the moment toward which he had been working for so long in absolute secrecy. No one—not even his wife, not his closest friend—could have any idea of what he had accomplished; and in the future, no one would ever suspect him. Who would think that he, of all people, had created the most perfect forgeries of £1 notes in history? The counterfeit bills in his wallet were indistinguishable from the real ones produced under the strictest security conditions by the Bank of England. To prove the quality of his handiwork, the forger had chosen the boldest possible demonstration. He would pass the notes himself, directly over the counter of this well-known bank.

When his turn came, the forger calmly extracted ten counterfeit £1 notes from his wallet, extended them toward the teller, and asked for two £5 notes in return. The teller took the £1 notes and counted them rapidly with expert fingers. The forger watched with what appeared to be only mild interest, permitting himself a slight smile as the teller put the forged £1s into a drawer and plucked out two genuine £5 notes.

"Thank you," the forger said as he took them. "Cheerio."

"Cheerio," the teller said.

Emerging from the bank, the forger fell into step with the crowd on this downtown sidewalk. He took a deep breath and tapped his wallet with a finger. He had just introduced ten undetectable counterfeit notes into the British economy, confirming what he had already known: the bills were, in fact, perfect. The photo-offset creations were nothing short of masterpieces. Having passed this initial test, the ten notes could be multiplied into thousands, even millions. The forger was equally certain of being able to produce higher and higher denominations—without ever being identified, much less caught.

With the dignity of a man always in complete control, he walked off and disappeared.

July 1972

Being new as well as undetectable, the forgeries were allowed into general circulation, first into the pockets of the bank's customers, then through stores, and out into the public's hands again. No citizen was "stuck" with a forged £1 note; instead, the bills trickled into the Bank of England, where electronic sorting machines "rejected" them.

The Bank's Printing Works issued an internal memorandum that confirmed the officials' worst fears: "None of these reproductions is a genuine Bank of England note, but each bears words, figures, letters, marks, lines, and devices peculiar to and used upon the one-pound Bank of England note. The reproductions have been printed by the offset-litho printing process, using several different printing plates, made from photographic positives and negatives produced by a separation and re-touching process. They are the result of a long and painstaking process involving a great deal of skill."

In fact, the notes were of a quality surpassing that of any forgeries produced in the century, with the single possible exception of the German "white fivers" produced by Hitler's order during World War II. The Nazis had planned to flood England with counterfeit £5 bills, hoping to undermine the British economy. Wounded by lack of confidence in the currency, the nation's monetary system presumably would falter and collapse amid public chaos.

The memory of Hitler's scheme gave officials at the Bank of England and Scotland Yard every reason to panic. The English were currently under siege once more, this time by the Irish Republican Army. Only five months before, IRA terrorists had exploded a bomb at the Aldershot army base near London, killing seven victims. The IRA claimed the blast was in retaliation for the recent killing of thirteen civilians in Londonderry by British paratroopers. Now there was official concern that IRA terrorists would attempt a major extension of their operations in England as well as Ulster. Could they also be planning to dump a blizzard of counterfeit currency?

A major concern was inflation. Because the notes were flawless, millions could be floated in public circulation without anyone's knowledge. A further-inflated economy would be ruinous, but eventually the truth would come out and all holders of bogus bills would suffer losses. Vast quantities could create a massive, sudden calamity with grave consequences for the nation.

Within a few weeks after the first £1 note was spotted, the Bank of England informed Scotland Yard that the rate of influx had jumped to nearly two hundred notes per day.

Soon it climbed to twice that much and, by summer, the Bank's scanning machines were rejecting more than two thousand per week; yet not a single counterfeit bill had been detected by the public or by a commercial bank. It was as if a hurricane were blowing up high seas against the walls of the vulnerable Bank, whose officials could only brace themselves for the tidal wave.

Pressure on the Yard was enormous. Could the forger be stopped? What kind of distribution system did he have? Was there a network of middlemen working its way down to street-level passers? If so, it would be impossible for detectives to retrace the notes up through the labyrinth, from one link to another, and reach the printer.

The Yard tripled its manpower on the case and placed each "known" forger under surveillance. All "snouts"— paid informers—were asked if they knew of any recent counterfeiting activity. Some had heard of a forged £1 note in circulation, but their information was vague and unhelpful.

Detectives had expected this response. It had been obvious from the beginning that these notes were the work of someone new. But what sort of man? Was he a figure in the British underworld or a lone individual? Was he connected to the IRA?

The Yard's frustration mounted daily. The Bank of England continued to report a growing influx of notes and, at the highest levels of government, there was agitation for detectives to come up with results before word of the crisis leaked to the public. Because no passers of the forged notes were being caught, there was not the slightest lead to be followed and developed. One informer mentioned that a forger nicknamed "the Magician" had vowed to "break the Bank of England," but so far it was just a rumor.

The Bank waited for action from the Yard, whose detectives had exhausted all possible avenues of investigation. There was high-level talk of recalling all the £1 notes and issuing a new design. The Bank's printing experts were already developing a new, smaller bill, with different patterns and more color; but to order a total cancellation of the current £1 denomination was tantamount to announcing the crisis and causing pandemonium. For the time being, there was little choice but to maintain the strictest secrecy and pray for a miracle.

21 August 1972

Newscasts in England and around the world reported that two men, a Scotsman and an American, had just made the first crossing of the Swiss and Italian Alps by hot-air balloon. The forger may or may not have seen the television films that evening; he may or may not have read the story in the papers the following day; but if he had, he might well have reacted with interest and admiration. The experts had previously believed that crossing the Alps in such a manner was an impossible feat, just as other experts had said that creating perfect forgeries of English currency was beyond anyone's capability.

The balloon was 120 feet high, containing 140,000 cubic feet of hot air. It had been piloted by Donald Cameron of Bristol and a New Yorker named Mark Yarry. The pair, in their early thirties, had waited a week in the Swiss mountain resort of Zermatt before the weather conditions were right. After taking off, the balloon skirted the Matterhorn and crossed directly over the 15,200-foot summit of Monte Rosa. The ride went smoothly except for one harrowing moment over a peak, when upslope winds bounced the balloon up and down like a Ping-Pong ball atop a water fountain. But in less than three hours of flight time, they landed at the small industrial town of Biella, Italy, in the midst of twenty thousand cheering spectators.

During the celebration, Mark Yarry told reporters that he was a "self-employed business consultant" from New York who had taken up ballooning "as a hobby" after seeing a special program about the sport on television.

"It was the most beautiful thing I'd ever seen," Yarry said. "It was so graceful and slow-moving. It seemed a marvelous way to fly."

But why had he chosen to try such a dangerous route?

"People never know their limitations," Yarry replied. "I intend to keep on testing my own."

The reporters then asked what other goals he had as a balloonist.

"To fly across the Atlantic," Yarry said.

But why?

"Because it's never been done before."

If the forger heard this news, he undoubtedly identified with the balloonists and their accomplishment. There was the workmanship involved in the making of the largest balloon in the world. To build it had required the same degree of inventiveness and skill that the forger had applied to the printing of his £1 notes. There was the preparation and precision needed to make the Alps crossing, involving months of research with top meteorologists, technicians, and scientists; but so, too, had the forger done his homework. As for the element of risk, he was facing as much as any balloonist did.

Moreover, the one-pounders had merely been a rehearsal for greater things; and he was ready now to close up shop until he began the next phase of his plan. It was time to retreat. While the public watched the television film of the balloon floating through the air, the forger reveled in his own triumph and temporarily went to ground.

1972–1974

Although the £1 notes continued to circulate freely, there was still no public awareness of the growing crisis. Just when England's monetary guardians were expecting an even greater surge of counterfeit bills, however, the rate of influx inexplicably began to drop. By the fall, the notes coming into the Bank were a mere trickle of the previous amounts; and by the end of 1972, only a handful were showing up each day.

The Yard made a last-ditch effort in its investigation, but it was clear that the mysterious forger had shut down his printing operation. The question was why—when he was at the peak of his success, in so untouchable a position— would he stop himself? A profitable "killing" would have been rather simple. But if the forger's motive wasn't to make as much money in the shortest possible time, what else could it be?

The notes dried up completely during 1973 and an exasperated Scotland Yard suspended its investigation. By the following year, IRA activity once again became the paramount problem for the British authorities. A full-scale security review was launched by the Government in early 1974. In June, a bomb exploded in the Houses of Parliament, damaging Westminster Hall; and then another bomb, this time at the Tower of London, killed one tourist and injured dozens of others. Home Secretary Roy Jenkins prepared to request emergency legislation that would outlaw the IRA and give police sweeping powers of arrest and detention.

On July 22, in the midst of the growing public panic over terrorist activities, the Bank of England reported to Scotland Yard that a new counterfeit note had been detected by the scanning machines—except that this time it was a fiver. Because of its workmanship, it had unquestionably been produced by the same forger, who had outdone himself by rising to the task of reproducing the various colors of the £5 note. The Yard reopened its investigation with a vengeance, but by September the notes were appearing at the rate of £50,000 per week. The Bank of England urged immediate action by the Yard to trace the source of the bills before the calamity became public knowledge; and the British Government, beset by bombs and economic crisis and now by this shocking new influx of forged currency, waited helplessly in anticipation of what was coming next.

Tuesday, 24 September 1974

Mark Yarry, the balloonist, was still planning with his friend Don Cameron to make the first Atlantic crossing. Meanwhile, a Connecticut-based American optical company had sent him to London in hopes that he could set up a European subsidiary. He and his wife, Monica, and their two small daughters had moved into a completely furnished, luxurious town house at 20 Wilton Place in the fashionable Knightsbridge-Belgravia district of the West End. The five-story house was two blocks from the Carlton Tower Hotel and just a city stroll from Harrods, the famous department store. The Yarrys had arrived at their new home in mid-September; and on this morning Mark set out for meetings at optical houses in various sections of London.

He was carrying a plain black satchel crammed with prototypes of eyeglass frames. His task was to line up as many lucrative orders as possible, worth a minimum of $50,000 each, so that the company could justify his expenses and quickly establish the London-based European office. It was nine o'clock in the morning. Faced with the prospect of lugging his heavy case around for the next eight hours, he decided to hire a taxicab for the day. He stood in front of the long, unbroken block of similar five-story houses and raised his free arm to hail a cab coming from his left.

It was a typical black London taxicab. The driver, perhaps thirty years old, gave a little nod and made a quick U-turn. He stopped in front of Mark, who stood waiting to speak to him through the window.

"Good morning," the driver said. His hair was prematurely gray and he had a bright smile and a warm, friendly expression. "Where to, guv?"

"Well," Mark said, "I have a bunch of calls to make. They're spread all over London. Could we arrange a flat fee for about eight hours? That way I won't be looking for a cab each time."

"Could cost a few quid, mate."

"How about twenty pounds?" Mark asked, but the driver stared at him without any reaction. "And a five-pound tip on top of the deal."

"With a break for lunch?"

"Sure. And while I'm in my meetings, you can go for tea or coffee."

"Sounds fine, mate."

Mark climbed into the spacious passenger section in the

rear. "The first stop is over in Mount Pleasant," he said as the driver headed off in the thick of the morning traffic. He sat back and they rode up the block to Knightsbridge, the street bordering the southern edge of Hyde Park, and turned right. The driver, who offered his name as Dave, sped past Hyde Park Corner and the Wellington Arch, to Piccadilly, and began the long ride east through downtown London.

"You're an American?" Dave asked.

"That's right. From New York."

"Here on business?"

"Yes, but I'm living here as well."

"Ah," Dave said. "That your 'ouse, then? Where I just picked you up?"

"That's right. My company rents it for me."

"Been 'ere long?"

"Only about ten days. But I've lived in England before. My family and I just moved back from the south of France."

"Sounds like you're a world traveler."

"Well, my wife's British. The first time here, we lived in Surrey."

"You don't say."

"We had a house in a place called Worplesdon."

"I know that area. Very nice."

"It was on eight acres," Mark went on, enjoying the pleasant chitchat and relaxing while Dave maneuvered through the traffic on this warm fall day. "We had two cottages in addition to the main house, and five in staff."

"Five? Must have a big family."

"No," Mark laughed, "just two kids. There was more in staff than there was of us!"

"Why'd you leave?" Dave asked. "The British weather? The food?"

"No, nothing like that. My wife and I had always wanted to live in the south of France. So we flew down to

14

Nice and rented a car and started looking at houses in Cannes."

"You preferred Cannes to Nice, eh?"

"Well, we discovered this village called Mougins. It's near Cannes and about twenty-five kilometers from Nice. A dream environment. Believe it or not, we found a beautiful little villa called Cinderella."

"The Villa Cinderella," Dave said.

"Swimming pool, rose garden—really an ideal place to live. My English wife is a real Francophile. Loves the whole atmosphere of Cannes and the Riviera."

"So why'd you come back to England?"

"Business," Mark said, but something made him hold back any further details. The morning newspaper had contained a report of homes being burglarized in the West End; and he realized for the first time that the cabdriver, in a very casual way, had been putting him through a kind of interrogation. Dave seemed friendly and genuinely curious, but was there anything else behind his questions? They rode the rest of the way to the first stop in silence.

By mid-afternoon, Mark was exhausted from his series of meetings, while the chitchat in the cab had been a way to relieve the tension. Dave was amiable, talkative, and well-informed. Between stops they had discussed a number of topics, from the weather to women to food to sports. Later, Dave had brought up the subject of inflation, displaying considerable insight into the woes of the British economy.

At around one o'clock they had taken a lunch break, Mark going off by himself to a pub. Now, after another meeting, they were on their way to a stop in Islington. Mark was talking about his interest in ballooning, mentioning that he flew airplanes as well.

"You have lots of 'obbies, eh?"

15

"Yes, I suppose I do," Mark said.

"What other ones?"

"Well, I'm a philatelist."

"Stamp collector?"

"Right."

"You buy valuable stamps?"

"A fair amount. Right now I'm collecting forgeries."

There was a brief silence. "Forgeries of stamps?"

"Un hunh. Some forgeries are worth more than the originals, because of their scarcity."

"I see," Dave said. He glanced around as if to say something else, but there was an awkward pause. He seemed to be debating with himself, so Mark waited in silence. At last Dave said, "Would you be interested in *other* types of forgeries?"

"Like what?"

"Well," Dave went on, again with obvious hesitation, "how about forged bank notes?"

"Counterfeit money?"

"Right. English five-pound notes."

"Well," Mark said, "I might be. I'd love to see the British five-pound note that the Germans made during the Second World War. I hear that was a brilliant piece of work."

"I know of some that are the finest ever produced."

"Really?" Mark asked, thinking that he might be prepared to spend up to £100 for a rare counterfeit bill. "How much do they sell for?"

"Two quid apiece."

"Two pounds," Mark said, but his voice trailed off and he fell silent. Two pounds? How could that be? By now, the German-produced forgeries had to be quite rare and expensive. They were collectors' items, worth a great deal. In other words, Dave must be talking about actual counterfeit money, the illegal stuff that you try to pass on the

16

street. I must have given him the impression that I'm open to that type of thing. He's taking a real chance, but he must feel we've established a rapport. . . .

What do I say now? Mark wondered. Out of impulse, he felt drawn to becoming more involved, not less. To express a lack of interest would run counter to his nature, which was most of all to be curious. Is this man really offering to sell me some bogus fivers?

"Well," he said at last, "I *could* be interested."

"How might that come about?"

Mark thought a moment, feeling as though he had suddenly been thrust into a scene out of some television series. The thing is, he thought, I'm *enjoying* it. He said, "Perhaps I could see some samples," surprising himself at the ease with which he had thought of making such a request.

"Okay, mate."

"I don't suppose you have any with you."

"No, but I can get 'em right away."

"Could you make a delivery?"

"Sure."

"How many?" Mark asked, his heart beginning to pound as he realized that he was already discussing an illegal transaction. He had no thought of actually going through with it, but he felt strangely compelled to play along and see what would happen next. If Dave figured him to be a potential buyer, why not assume the role for a while?

"A couple," Dave was saying. "If you want to see samples, I'll bring you two."

"All right," Mark said, but now he felt the urge, even the need, to build up his credibility. "If the samples are really good, I might be interested in a large quantity."

"These notes are the best, mate. The best."

"You have access to a lot?"

"Any amount you want, mate."

The taxicab took a zigzagging route through London as Mark checked off each stop on his itinerary. He had planned his meetings with executives of the optical industry so that he would finish near home in the West End. There was no further discussion of forged money, although now all their topics of conversation seemed to take on double meanings. Improvising, Mark tried to convey by innuendo that he was some sort of a wheeler-dealer who moved in fast circles. He talked about gambling casinos in Monte Carlo and the Bahamas, adding as an afterthought that when he had lived in England previously he had joined the Clermont Club, where he was fond of the roulette wheel. Mark had visited all these places during his travels and, in a flight of fantasy, he also alluded to "certain business associates in Miami," leaving Dave to use his own imagination to fill in the blanks. The more Mark talked in this fashion, the less fear he felt. When they pulled into Wilton Place at five-thirty in the afternoon, he was thoroughly relaxed, enjoying the character that he'd adopted.

"What's your name, mate?"

"Mark."

They were still in the cab, the motor running. "Here's your twenty pounds," Mark said, "and the five on top."

Dave took the bills matter-of-factly. "When would you like to see the samples?"

Hesitating, Mark thought he should give himself some time. He was curious to see the quality of the £5 notes, but what then? "How about the day after tomorrow?" he said.

"Fine."

"But come in the morning, because I have a busy schedule."

"Ten o'clock?"

"Okay. Just ring the bell."

Dave turned to face him directly. "You won't be disappointed."

Mark stared back. "I don't expect to be."

"Cheerio," Dave said.

"Good-bye."

The top three floors at 20 Wilton Place contained bedrooms, while on ground level were a kitchen and a lovely dining room that looked out over the street. The next high-ceiling level had a large drawing room facing both front and back, but there was also a study that Mark used as an office. Too keyed up to eat dinner, he had come here to be alone. . . .

Perhaps most men would have let the matter rest after a few minutes of quiet reflection, but such was not Mark Yarry's way of relating to the world around him. He was the type, for example, who might hop a plane to the Fiji Islands within hours of it having crossed his mind. Notions that came into his head, from whatever source, were immediately translated into active fantasizing, then into fierce desire, then into the action itself. Practical concerns about money and time and other consequences were usually forgotten as he moved ahead on his sudden, single-minded course. It helped that his wife had been an airline flight attendant, accustomed to traveling the world on her own, so that he often was able to join her in some foreign city or at least know that she was seldom stuck at home too long by herself. For both of them, running to an airport was a way of life.

But there were other ways to take flight—more ways than as a balloonist. To Mark, no profession was ever impossible to take up; no field of interest seemed too complicated or overwhelming. His response to almost anything was, more often than not, "I can do that"; or "This problem can be solved"; or, simply, "Why not?" The fantasies were fueled by a supreme confidence that he could make them real; and the delight in proving it, the challenge of trying, was reward enough. As a youngster, for example, he had smuggled himself aboard a cargo plane that flew him from New York to Paris.

As an adult, Mark had joined an array of business ventures, although for a five-year span he had settled into the executive vice-presidency of the *Institutional Investor,* one of Wall Street's prestigious financial publications. He had been highly successful selling ad space for the magazine, largely because he was able to convey his own enthusiasm and motivate others to share it. Most of all, he loved to talk, to tell stories and dazzle his listeners with tales of intrigue and adventure. With a mind that retained all sorts of impressions, facts, and figures, he could weave a spell over most any group of friends or strangers. And with an ear for accents and dialect, he was able to impersonate the characters in his stories as he went along. In the true sense of the word, he was a raconteur.

Even at this moment, in the study of his rented house in Knightsbridge, Mark could already imagine himself spinning out the yarn he had only begun to experience: "There I was, in London, and I hailed a taxi. Next thing I knew . . ." and so forth, leading to this particular point in the tale, when the lead character is faced with a decision to pursue or not to pursue . . .

The study was small and cozy, lined on all sides with floor-to-ceiling bookshelves that were completely filled. It had a couch, two easy chairs, a coffee table, and a desk facing the window, which overlooked a courtyard. In one of the easy chairs, Mark sipped some brandy and wondered what the best course of action was. A man was coming to the door on Thursday morning with samples of counterfeit English money, expecting him to order a large quantity. What now?

Well, he could simply look at the bills, satisfy his curiosity, and decline to make the purchase. No problem. But what if he turned around and went to the police? Perhaps the adventure could be stretched a bit further, providing a new experience. If nothing else, it would be interesting to see what response he might get. But, he wondered, do I call the London police or the American embassy? Well, I'm a foreigner, so I might as well call my own people and let them report it.

When he reached the United States embassy, Mark was put through to a guard on night duty. "What can I do for you?"

"Well," Mark said into the phone, "my name is Yarry. I'm an American living in London. I was just offered some counterfeit five-pound notes for sale."

"We can't handle that."

"You can't?"

"It's not our jurisdiction. Why don't you call Scotland Yard?"

"I figured you would do that for me."

"Better if you call 'em direct. Want the number?"

"Okay, sure," Mark muttered. He took down Scotland Yard's number and hung up. Should I go on with this? he wondered. Why don't I just forget the whole thing? Oh, well, he thought as he picked up the phone and dialed again, what can I lose?

"Good evening. This is Scotland Yard."

"My name is Mark Yarry. I'm an American citizen and I want to report that someone has offered to sell me some counterfeit English money."

"I'll put you through to C-1 Reserve."

"All right, fine."

A few moments later, a sergeant came on the line. "Can I help you, sir?"

Mark went through the story again and was told that someone from the forgery squad would be in touch with him first thing the following morning. The forgery squad, he thought with delight. "There I was, waiting for Scotland Yard to make contact with me . . ."

Wednesday, 25 September

Detective Constable James Goldie, thirty-four, had been part of the National Central Office for the Suppression of Counterfeit Currency (known simply as the forgery squad) at New Scotland Yard for several months. A former professional football player, Jim was still heavily involved with the sport as a player-coach on the Metropolitan Police team. After just six weeks on the forgery squad, he broke his leg while playing a game in Trowbridge, Wiltshire, and was laid up for nearly six months. Now he was back at the Yard after only a few weeks and still had the least experience with counterfeit currency of any officer on the squad.

On this particular morning, he stepped off the elevator on the second floor and poked his head into the Central Liaison Office. At the switchboard was a drug-squad officer named Tom Anderson, and the two men passed some time in friendly conversation. "By the way," Anderson said as Jim was about to move on, "there was a call last night from a Yank. Says he was offered a forged five-pound note."

Jim Goldie reacted with typical reserve, showing almost no emotion on his face. He had heard all the commotion about the forged £5 notes in circulation—in fact, he'd been given a special briefing upon his return to the Yard—and he knew that his colleagues were racing around trying to find some leads.

"You have the number and address?" Jim asked.

"Right here—it's on Wilton Place."

At his desk, Jim placed the call and found himself speaking to a woman with an English accent. He asked for Mr. Yarry and waited until the American came on the line.

"Mr. Yarry? This is Detective Constable Goldie from New Scotland Yard."

"Hi. Thanks for calling back. Look, I don't know if this is very important, but yesterday a cabdriver offered to sell me some counterfeit five-pound notes."

"Did you get his name?"

"He introduced himself as Dave."

"That's it?"

"Well, he's coming around tomorrow morning with a couple of samples."

Jim waited for an explanation. "Samples?"

"I sort of played along with him. I'm not even sure why."

As the conversation continued, Jim made arrangements to stop at 20 Wilton Place later in the morning. He also made a mental note that Mr. Yarry seemed quite straightforward, candidly admitting that he had expressed interest in buying forged currency "out of sheer impulse." Perhaps most people would have backed away from the offer entirely, but this chap apparently had played along for the fun of it. An unusual way to behave, but just possibly an important break for the Yard.

When he arrived in Knightsbridge shortly before eleven, Jim reminded himself that the neighborhood was among the highest priced in London. Here was Sloane Street, with its fashionable flats and stores, and Beauchamp Place, with its famous antique shops. At one end of Wilton Place, toward Hyde Park, was the modern Berkeley Hotel, one of the finest places to stay in the entire city; and, Jim knew, the luxury town houses along Wilton Place and Wilton Crescent were occupied by wealthy people from all over the world. It was clear that Mr. Yarry was no ordinary American. Most likely, the cabdriver named Dave had made the same assessment.

The row of houses on Wilton Place had black-iron fences running along the sidewalk in front of their little stucco patios. The doors of the houses varied in color—green, stained wood, dark blue—and most had tiny balconies or terraces jutting out from the second floor, overlooking the patios. The black door of No. 20 was about two-thirds into the block from Hyde Park. Diagonally across the street was the nineteeth-century Saint Paul's, Knightsbridge, and directly opposite was another row of expensive, five-story homes. Near the crescent-shaped park at the far end of the little street, the pavement widened to provide room for taxicabs to park. The weather had turned somewhat chilly, but the sun was shining and the entire neighborhood, with its open spaces and restored buildings, seemed to sparkle with style, culture, and money.

Jim rang the doorbell. Mark Yarry was in his mid-thirties, wearing a tan cashmere jacket with a shirt open at the collar. He was about five feet ten, slim and ruggedly handsome, with brown hair and eyes, and a warm, easy smile.

"I'm Detective Constable Goldie from the Yard."

Mark let him into the hall and closed the door. "Can I see some identification?"

Jim produced a Metropolitan Police identification card and watched as Yarry carefully studied it.

"I'm glad you're in plainclothes," Yarry said, referring to Jim's dark, three-piece suit. "I mean, for all I know somebody's out there watching the house."

In the ground-floor dining room, Yarry's attractive wife served some coffee. Jim was impressed by the splendor of the furnishings and by the presence of a housekeeper and a live-in nanny who took care of the two children. The formal dining room was dominated by a George III table with twelve high-backed chairs and an elegant chandelier suspended from the ceiling. There were two matching corner-wall cabinets, plus a large serving table, and the magnificent furniture contained an assortment of sparkling silverware on display. Also, Jim noticed, a large, expensive-looking Oriental carpet covered much of the highly polished oak floor.

Taking notes, he listened as Mark described his daylong experience with Dave, the cabdriver, adding, "We got into a discussion of forged stamps."

"Why?"

"I'm a philatelist. One of my specialties is forgeries."

"How did the counterfeit five-pound notes come up?"

Mark explained how Dave had suddenly mentioned forged bank notes.

"I thought he was talking about the old German forgery," he said. "I asked him how much and he said two quid apiece. Well, I knew right away, by the price, that he was referring to *real* counterfeit money, so to speak. My mind went temporarily blank. What do you say to a guy who's offering you funny money?"

"What *did* you say?"

"I told him I'd like to see some samples."

"I still don't comprehend why," Jim said.

"Well, do you know the saying that in every man there's a little bit of Walter Mitty? In my case, there's a lot of

Walter Mitty. And besides, I wouldn't mind seeing how good those notes are."

"He told you they're good?" Jim asked.

"Oh, yes. He said they're the 'finest ever produced.' "

"Well, the Yard's objective is putting any forger out of business, and there *is* a dangerous note in circulation. It's almost totally undetectable. We'd very much like to find the source."

"How can I help?"

"You already have," Jim said.

"Listen, I told him I might want to purchase a *large* amount. He didn't bat an eye. He said he could supply me with any quantity I want."

Jim looked at him a moment. "Why'd you ask for a large amount?"

"I told you—I was just going along, playing the role. It seemed like the natural thing to say. He had the impression that I'm fairly well-heeled, so I just acted the way he expected."

Jim silently tried to put himself in the cabdriver's position. Through Dave's eyes, Yarry must have seemed a logical buyer. Here was a slim chance to make headway in the investigation. "Well," he said at last, "it's probable that this bloke won't turn up tomorrow morning. But just in case he does, I'd like to be here."

"Sure. What's the plan?"

"I have to speak to my governor," Jim said as they walked to the door. Outside, he tried to suppress a great wave of excitement. This one tiny lead was more than any other detective had come up with. The idea was to stay calm, go by the book, follow it up one step at a time.

At Scotland Yard, Jim went to the head of the forgery squad, Superintendent John Miller, and reported what

Yarry had told him. Miller seemed enthusiastic. The main job, he emphasized, was to capture the forger *and* seize the photographic negatives, the printing plates, and the machinery with which he was producing the notes. It was no use arresting a passer or even a middleman or high-level distributor unless, in the end, the printer himself was stopped.

Superintendent Miller also said that a top priority was to "get the American out of it" as soon as possible. It was never good police procedure to involve a private citizen in any criminal investigation. It meant that the Yard would lose control over events; and, besides, it was dangerous. In this case, Yarry was not only a civilian but a foreigner, inviting international complications. The headlines—"American Killed While Helping Scotland Yard"—could be a disaster.

The key task was to remove Yarry quickly and introduce a Yard operative who would take over. The undercover agent would assume the role of Yarry's top-level contact and try to reach the printer.

"Go see if the cabbie shows up," Miller said. "If he does, have C-11 take his photograph."

That evening, Jim studied some of the forged £5 notes, which had been designated as the "D.5/2" by the Yard. According to various memoranda, the Bank of England was still reporting an influx of ten thousand notes per week. The bills certainly could pass as the real thing, although the complicated design of the fiver must have been incredibly difficult to reproduce. On the front were two drawings in addition to the portrait of the Queen, plus complicated patterns, lines, letters, and numbers. On the back was a portrait of the Duke of Wellington and a representation of the Battle of Waterloo. Moreover, each English £5 note had several colors, including magenta, yellow, blue, and brown, with various shadings. Such a bill was almost impossible to re-create, yet the forger had done so. He had even photographed and printed the vertical "security" thread of thin metal imbedded in the official note paper, seen when the bill is held up to light; although, of course, he had been unable to duplicate the metal itself, which was why the bank's electronic sorters had "rejected" the bills.

According to the Yard's experts, there were at least fifty different serial numbers among the counterfeit bills which had turned up at the Bank of England. The forger had been forced to use regular paper instead of a more durable kind produced exclusively, and under top-secret conditions, for the Bank. Even so, it took Jim practice to be able to feel a specimen of the D.5/2 note with his fingers and distinguish it from a genuine bill.

Thursday, 26 September

In the morning Jim Goldie drove to Knightsbridge and met with Detective Douglas Filbey of C-11, who would stay outside and attempt to get the cabdriver's license and registration numbers as well as his photograph. Jim rang the bell at 20 Wilton Place shortly after nine. Mark greeted him, saying that he'd been up since six, having consumed several cups of coffee and smoked an entire pack of cigarettes. His two daughters—Samantha, age six, and Melissa, age four—had already been taken to the Lycée Français de Londres, where they had been enrolled so they could continue the French education they had begun during the past year. Monica was on her way to visit art galleries and a jewelry shop in nearby Belgravia.

From the ground-floor dining room, Jim and Mark observed the activity on the street. "If he shows up," Jim said, "just take the samples and tell him to come back tomorrow. Explain you need time to look them over."

Mark nodded. "Do you think he's the forger?"

"Probably not. But he might be a direct link. That's what we're hoping. Tell him you've got a contact who's going to supply the money for one large purchase. You want a face value of one hundred thousand pounds. That way, we might be able to introduce an undercover agent who can negotiate directly with the Magician."

"The who?"

"The Magician. We've heard that's his nickname."

"Sounds intriguing," Mark said.

"The idea is that our man will take over as the money supplier."

"Why don't I do it myself?"

"Impossible. We'd have to rewrite the Yard's entire rule book. By the way," Jim continued, "when we first spoke on the phone you said you're in the optical business."

"That's right."

"Does the cabdriver know that?"

"I had a heavy black bag full of prototype eyeglass frames, but for all he knew I was carrying guns."

"So he doesn't know what to make of you. Except that you can afford a pretty good life-style."

"He has the impression that I know my way around in the world. I deliberately allowed him to infer that."

As they drank more coffee and waited, Jim answered a number of Mark's questions about the investigation. He kept his replies brief, stressing the seriousness of the matter while trying not to reveal too many specifics. From the Yard's point of view, Mark could be working for the Magician, attempting to find out how much progress the detectives had made; although in Jim's opinion, this unusual American was genuinely eager to help. Perhaps he *was* a Walter Mitty type whose fantasies overtook reality.

"He's here," Mark said.

Glancing out the window, Jim saw a black taxicab pull into Wilton Place. "I'll be upstairs," he said. "Good luck."

"God!" Mark shouted. "I've got to clear away these coffee cups!"

While Mark raced into the kitchen, Jim bounded up to the second-floor drawing room.

Dave was at the door with both hands in the pockets of his dark-blue windbreaker. "Good morning," Mark said. "Why don't you come in?"

They went into the dining room, Mark leading the way and trying to remember any television shows about counterfeiters. He could not recall a single line of dialogue that might be appropriate for this situation.

"Coffee?"

Dave stood there, a confident expression in his eyes, and said, "Sure," as he removed a hand from his windbreaker. He was holding what appeared to be two £5 notes.

Mark took the bills while staring at him, then moved away to examine them in the light of the window. My God, he thought, they're real! The guy is giving me two genuine £5 notes as "samples" in hopes that I'll place an order, but the actual counterfeit bills are probably terrible! What does he think I am, a jackass?

Placing the two bills on the table, he withdrew his wallet and pulled out one of his own £5 notes. As Dave took a seat, Mark picked up one of the "forgeries" and tried to make a comparison. Well, he thought, there's no difference. This isn't counterfeit money.

He turned to Dave. "Very nice."

Dave's face broke into a wide grin. "I told you they were perfect. How many would you like?"

"If I place an order, I'll want no less than a face value of a hundred thousand pounds," Mark said as he served the coffee.

"No problem."

"But I have to show these to my contact."

"Contact?"

"I've got a guy who'll supply the money. I never use my own, if I can help it."

"When are you going to see him?"

"I'll try to meet with him today or tonight. Why don't you come back here tomorrow at the same time?"

"And you'll have a 'yes' or a 'no' for me?"

"Right. I'm not fooling around. I want to do it clean and quick," Mark went on, feeling his way into the role. "If my contact likes what he sees, money is no object."

Dave sipped his coffee in silence, then stood up. "See you tomorrow," he said at last. "Same time?"

"Good."

When he had gone, Mark watched through the window until the cab disappeared down the block. He turned and raced upstairs to the drawing room to see Jim Goldic.

"It's a big rip-off," Mark said. "Look at these—they're real!"

Jim studied one of the bills, feeling it with his fingers and holding it up to the light. Mark observed that the detective had a calm, placid manner. He was about six feet one, carrying a trim, athletic body of perhaps one hundred and eighty pounds. He had bright brown eyes and reddish, sandy hair that grew in a mass of curls. He seemed anything but impulsive; yet now his face lit up and he exclaimed, "This is it! We've got it!"

"What do you mean?"

31

Jim turned to him, his Scotsman's face red from excitement. "These are the notes we're looking for."

"They're counterfeit?"

"This is the D.5/2."

"The what?"

"It's our code for this stuff. When is Dave coming back?"

"Tomorrow morning."

"Can I use your phone?"

"Sure," Mark said. He could not help but respond to Jim's emotion. The guy is really turned on, he thought. It was as if the room were filled with electricity, and Mark felt himself at the very center of the current.

On the telephone, Jim was matter-of-fact again. "The man made the delivery," he said. "It's what we want."

"All right," Superintendent Miller replied. "Is Yarry there?"

Jim looked over at Mark, who was studying one of the forged bank notes. "Yes. He's right here."

"We've got to get him out of this immediately and put our own man in."

"The cabdriver is coming back here tomorrow," Jim said.

"So we need Yarry's help for at least one more meeting."

"I'd say so. Definitely."

"Okay," Miller said. "I'm coming over there to check him out. This is very delicate. How much do you know about him?"

"Not much," Jim admitted.

"It could be a setup. He might be working with the forger."

"Yes, but I don't think so."

"He could have the house wired," Miller persisted.

"I don't think that's the case, sir."

"I'll be over there soon, Jim. Don't come back to the Yard. From now on, this is your assignment. Forget everything else."

Detective Filbey had jotted down the cab's license number and also had taken a photograph of Dave. Within a few hours, the Yard would have a complete rundown of his identity, background, and any criminal record. From here on, the coordination between Jim Goldie in the field and the officers at headquarters would be known as Operation Wellington, in reference to the Iron Duke.

Jim's colleagues at the Yard were by no means optimistic that Operation Wellington would get very far. As long as Jim was forced to rely on a private citizen—a foreigner, at that—there was little prospect of reaching the Magician and luring him into the open. The American might be able to arrange and receive a delivery by some distributor, which would give detectives a chance to seize the counterfeit currency but would leave them just as far away from the forger as they were at the moment.

Jim's immediate concern was to motivate Mark in the right direction, to maintain his willingness to help while keeping him under tight control. At this moment, he had to make sure Mark didn't become so afraid that he'd want to back out.

"My governor is coming over," Jim said. "His name is John Miller. Head of the forgery squad. He wants to meet you."

"Look, how do I know that people aren't out there watching the house?"

"He'll be in plainclothes, so nobody can suss him out as the Old Bill."

"Pardon?"

"There's no way anybody would discover that he's a police officer," Jim explained.

"But maybe he should come dressed as a house painter or something."

"No need for that. For all anybody knows, he could be one of your business associates."

"Just so long as he doesn't come over here in a damn raincoat and hat, the way you see these Scotland Yard detectives in the movies. I mean, the sun is shining out there."

"Don't worry," Jim said.

They heard the doorbell ring. The housekeeper answered and they could hear Superintendent Miller's voice below. Jim followed Mark to the head of the stairs. Climbing toward them was Miller in a gray, wrinkled raincoat.

"Oh, shit," Mark muttered, as Jim rolled his eyes upward.

Miller strode into the second-floor study in a businesslike manner and, without taking off his raincoat, plopped into a chair. In his fifties, Miller was a total professional, distrustful of civilians and skeptical by training and experience. He viewed Mark's involvement as a necessary evil to be tolerated until the Yard could maneuver its own man into position.

Jim went over the details while Miller examined the two sample forgeries. The superintendent took out a notepad and pen, then glanced at Mark. "May I have your full name, sir?"

"Mark Robert Yarry."

"Age?"

"Thirty-four."

"United States citizen?"

"That's right."

"Can I see your passport?"

"Just a second."

Mark opened a desk drawer in the study and pulled out his passport. Miller copied down the number and leafed through the pages, noticing all the entries. "You do a lot of traveling, eh?"

"A fair amount."

"What sort of business are you in?"

"At the moment I'm with an optical-import firm based in Connecticut."

"What do you mean at the moment?"

"Look, if you're worried about my background, why don't you check with the FBI?"

"We already have. They're sending us a report."

"Good," Mark said evenly. "So why are you asking me all these questions?"

"Mr. Yarry, your credibility as a witness could be very important, if we ever have a case and go to trial. We have to know everything there is to know about you."

"I understand, but if you recall, *I* notified *you* about this situation."

"And we're grateful, sir."

"Furthermore," Mark said, his voice rising a bit, "I feel uncomfortable. You seem to think *I'm* the criminal. Believe me, I really can't afford to spend my time like this. I thought I was doing you a favor."

"I understand," Miller said. "We may need your help for just a few more days, until we can introduce our own undercover agent to take your place."

"The sooner the better," Mark said.

"Meanwhile," Miller went on, rising abruptly from his chair and heading for the door, "you'll get all instructions from Officer Goldie, here. Good day, sir."

Mark walked into the drawing room and paced around until Jim joined him. "Maybe I'll back out of this whole thing," Mark said. "I don't need any third degree."

"He's just being cautious," Jim said.

"Well, his whole attitude is that I'm some sort of criminal informer. He parades in here like God and talks *down* to me. I have a family and it could be in danger! If he wants me to put my neck on the line, the least he can do is treat me as an honest citizen."

"It's his manner. Don't judge all of Scotland Yard by only one man."

"If he doesn't trust me, I don't want to continue."

"It's just not a typical situation."

"Then he shouldn't act in a typical way!"

"Let's start all over again," Jim pleaded. "This is a very important case. We're in a national emergency. The Yard is under great pressure—we've got to get these notes out of circulation. We need your help."

"Well, I'd rather not work with a pompous guy like that."

"You don't have to. *I'm* your contact, remember? I'm assigned to work with you on an exclusive basis until we can get our own man into it. I'm not even supposed to show my face at the Yard."

"Sounds like you and Miller are playing a 'good-guy–bad-guy' routine, like on television."

"No, no, no. He's the head of the squad. He *has* to be cautious, even skeptical. But from now on, he has to rely on me. Whatever I tell him, that's what he'll go on," Jim said, realizing that he'd suddenly been thrust into the role of a buffer between Mark Yarry and Scotland Yard. He would have to stand between the two, gaining the trust and confidence of each, to get this case off the ground. It wouldn't be easy.

Friday,
27 September

Dave's taxicab pulled into Wilton Place right on time. Jim concealed himself in the upstairs drawing room. He had instructed Mark to express reservations about the quality of the counterfeit bills and request additional samples. It might strengthen his credibility as a buyer; and, just as essential, it might increase Dave's impatience to make a deal.

Mark was less than enthusiastic about the delaying tactic. Since meeting Dave and making the call to the Yard, he had been unable to put total energy into his work. He had uprooted his family from the south of France, where they had lived only eight months, solely for the challenge of setting up a London office for his company. He and Monica had shared mixed feelings about leaving the idyllic atmosphere of Cannes. To make the move to England more palatable for his wife, he had chosen the Knightsbridge-Belgravia section. Monica would be in the most attractive environment possible, within walking distance to quality shops and restaurants. The company, believing in Mark's ability based on his past record, had agreed to pay a total expense bill of more than $4000 a month for the house and maintenance. If he failed to achieve the desired results, he would find himself out of a lucrative job.

Yet he could not help being excited about his secret role for the Yard. Here was the kind of challenge that most men took up only in their daydreams. So far he had told Monica only that he was "doing a favor" for the Yard, and that she should simply "act naturally" while any strangers were in the house. On her part, Monica was determined to stay as far in the background as possible.

"Good morning," Mark said as he greeted Dave at the door.

The young man came right to the point when he had stepped inside: "Do you want to place an order?"

"I need more samples," Mark said as they moved into the dining room.

"What for? You could see for yourself that they're the best."

"Well, my people say it's impossible to judge the quality on just two notes."

"But those models are perfect."

"It's out of my hands. If you can bring three more samples, we might be in business."

"All right," Dave said without concealing his disgust. "I'll bring you three more models on Monday at noon. But that's the end of it."

Monday, 30 September

Dave reappeared shortly after noon with the three additional notes. The Yard had done a thorough investigation of his background, but had found no record of criminal activity or associations. Dave was thirty years old, married, and living in the East End. He had been driving a cab for seven years. It was unlikely that he was the Magician, but as a middleman his credentials were impeccable. The police would never have sought him as a possible suspect.

With Jim Goldie positioned upstairs and unable to see or hear anything, Mark led Dave into the dining room. He took the three fake bills and examined them. These, too, were the product of such fine workmanship that he could not distinguish them from genuine bills.

" 'Far as I'm concerned," he said, "we have a deal. I don't see any problem. As I mentioned before, I want a face value of a hundred thousand pounds. That's twenty thousand notes. But they've got to be the same quality as the models."

"Fine," Dave said. "Now I have to put you together with the top man."

Mark's first reaction was disappointment that Dave was not, after all, the Magician; but he was also heartened by the prospect of getting to him soon. He said just the opposite: "Why do I have to do that? I don't care about seeing the top man. Why can't I deal just with you?"

"I'm his contact," Dave said. "I can't deliver such a large amount by myself."

"Look, I want to get this thing over with! I'm ready to buy the stuff right now!"

"I'll pick you up tomorrow," Dave said. "I'll come by at nine o'clock in the morning and you'll meet the head man. He's a genius. He—"

"I don't care what the hell he is. Can he sell me what I want or not?"

"Of course he can."

As soon as Dave had gone, Mark rushed upstairs to announce that he had an appointment to meet the Magician.

It had all happened too fast. There was no time to replace Mark with an undercover man from the Yard. For Jim Goldie, it meant having to ring his superiors and explain that the Magician was expecting to meet the American, not some new "money supplier" whose role could be played by a plainclothesman. Mark was going to be picked up tomorrow morning by Dave, who would take him to the meeting. Should there be a tail? No, Jim replied. If the go-betweens discovered they were being followed, Mark could be in immediate danger. It was best to let him go by himself, even though there was a risk.

Although he was aware that by all logic he should be wary if not thoroughly frightened, Mark fought to push aside any second thoughts. Maybe I'm nuts to even *think* of doing this, he said to himself, but then he became fired with anticipation. As the time drew near, his anxiety was counterbalanced by the thought of trying to match wits with this "genius" of a forger. He was certain that he could lure the Magician into the hands of the police.

Tuesday,
1 October

From the drawing-room window, Jim saw the taxicab make a U-turn and stop in front of the house. Moments later he saw Mark walk from the house and climb into the backseat. When the cab disappeared up the block, Jim turned away feeling helpless. Now all he could do was wait.

In the cab, Mark was silent as Dave drove to the end of Wilton Place and turned onto Knightsbridge. When they were passing Hyde Park Corner, Dave turned his head briefly and said, "I've vouched for you."

"What do you mean?"

"I told the man you're on the level. I said you could be trusted."

"Good."

"He asked me how long I've known you. I told him a couple of months."

"Why'd you say that? It's only been a week."

"He's very cautious. He wouldn't go for it if I told him the truth. I just took a chance on you. I feel you're trustworthy, but it would be hard to make him understand. Better to tell him we met a couple of months ago and that I've been doing some driving for you."

It was a crucial lie. In the forger's mind, Mark thought, my credibility is at least halfway established.

"Well, Dave, I don't think it was necessary to lie to him. But I'll cover you and go along with it."

"I appreciate it, mate."

"Call me 'Mark.' "

The taxi continued east to the curb on Piccadilly outside the Green Park underground station, near the Ritz Hotel. A slim man in his late forties, with dark hair and an angular, bony face came over to the cab and peered inside at Mark. He had a distrustful expression, but after a few seconds he jumped in and slammed the door.

"Drive," the man ordered.

Dave stepped on the gas to join the flow of traffic and said, "Mark, this is Ron."

"Hello," Mark said, sensing that the man was already suspicious of him.

"What do you want?" Ron shot back in thick, East End cockney tones. He was extremely tense, breathing heavily, and it seemed that he was on the verge of an angry explosion.

"I want to do business," Mark said in a slightly nervous tone.

"What do you have in mind?" Ron pressed.

"What are you offering?"

"Tell me your opinion of what you've seen."

"It's very good work."

Ron said evenly, "I can offer you any amount you want."

"At what price?" Mark asked, forcing himself to get into the role.

"I thought that was already settled. Dave says he told you two quid per note."

"Yes, but—"

"And you agreed," Ron insisted.

"All I said was that I'm interested," Mark replied, and it suddenly occurred to him that he had received no instructions about how he should bargain as a potential buyer. Well, he thought, I'll play hard to get. "I like the models very much, but I'm expecting a bulk rate. With the quantity I'm talking about, your price is much too high."

"Not for the quality."

"The quality is fine. It's just that two pounds is very expensive for the amount I'm buying."

"You told Dave that you want twenty thousand pieces?"

"That's right. A face value of one hundred thousand pounds, and no less. And for that amount, the maximum price I'm prepared to pay is a pound and a half," Mark said, surprised and pleased at how his credibility seemed to grow as he took the hard line.

"One pound fifty per note? No, no, no," Ron said, his face reddening. "The notes are too good for that."

"It doesn't matter how damn good the notes are. For the kind of quantity I'm buying, even a pound and a half is top money. There are excessive costs in distribution that have to be considered," Mark added, while a voice in his head asked, Where did *that* come from?

"Well, I can't sell 'em to you at such a low price."

Mark wondered how far he should go in playing the big shot. Was it time to stop resisting and give in? On impulse he decided to play it out: "Then the deal is off. Sorry we can't do business, Ron."

Dave continued driving through the West End. Once in

a while he made a sudden U-turn, apparently as a precaution against being followed. Ron had a furious expression in his eyes, as if at any moment he might turn on Mark in a rage.

"I can't go along with one pound fifty," he said at last. "Only the Magician can do that."

Here we go again, Mark thought. "The who?" he asked.

"The forger. The man who prints the notes."

"I thought *you* were the top man," Mark replied without concealing his frustration.

"I am. But the Magician sets the rules."

"Well, where is he? Let me talk to him."

"Nobody talks to him but me," Ron said. "I'll tell him your offer and get back to you if we have a deal."

"Just tell him to stop thinking so small. I'm offering to buy twenty thousand pieces of worthless paper."

"Worthless? What do you mean? They—"

"I mean they're worth only what I can make in terms of profit," Mark said. "In the meantime, I'm guaranteeing your man thirty thousand pounds! In *real* money."

"All I can do is talk to him."

"Tell your man it's simple arithmetic. I'd be lucky to make a profit of fifty pence per note," Mark ad-libbed.

"I'll tell him," Ron said. "But he's very proud. He'll probably say no."

As the cab slowed to a stop in front of 20 Wilton Place, Mark casually invited the two men inside for some coffee. Perhaps Ron would be impressed by the affluent surroundings and make a special plea to the forger to go ahead with the transaction.

Monica Yarry played the gracious hostess for the two members of the counterfeiting ring as they sat down at the dining-room table.

When Dave went to use the bathroom, Ron turned to Mark and said in a low voice, "How long have you known him?"

"Oh, about two months," Mark lied in a casual manner. "He's been driving me around, here and there."

Ron's tension seemed to subside and he started talking about various "jobs" he had "pulled off" in recent years, dropping the names of several well-publicized British crime figures. As Dave returned to the table, the cockney was describing how he had done a particular "job" for "some people over in the States, down in Miami."

Not to be outdone, Mark countered with a fabricated story about a "friend" of his named "Frankie the Cuban," also in Miami. "Do you know him?" Mark asked.

"Can't say I do," Ron said. "Frankie the Cuban? Never heard of him."

"I only call him when I need him," Mark said.

As the cryptic verbal sparring continued, Mark slipped deeper into his role as a man with "connections" all over the world. With a light, off-hand attitude, he tried to keep pace with Ron to prevent him from gaining the upper hand. But suddenly the cockney turned on him in anger: "You're a pretty big talker, but *we*'re the ones who've shown the goods!"

"Hey," Mark shot back. "I don't like taking orders. Are you threatening me?"

"When I threaten you, you'll know it," Ron retorted. "Let's just see the color of *your* money."

"You want to see it? Come back tomorrow."

"What's wrong with right now?"

"I don't keep a lot of cash around the house. But give me twenty-four hours and I'll have it."

Ron stood up, signaling to Dave that they were leaving. "I'll be back tomorrow afternoon around three," he said.

"Okay, but go talk to this Magician or whatever he is,

and tell him I've got thirty thousand pounds for one quick deal. If he doesn't want it, the whole thing is off."

"By the way," Ron said, "who's upstairs?"

Had Jim Goldie made a noise? "That's the housekeeper," Mark said.

Jim listened eagerly as Mark related the morning's events. He was grateful that there had been no violence, and amazed at how carefully Mark had played his role. It was clear that the man relished every moment when he was "onstage," so to speak. It was also apparent that the impulsive American had become committed to Operation Wellington.

"I'm gonna get to the Magician," Mark said. "I *know* I can bring him out in the open."

One surprise for Jim was that Mark had "negotiated" with Ron over the price of the notes. "Why did you do that?"

"Well, I felt I should negotiate *something*. I'm playing hard to get."

"But how did you come up with one pound fifty per note?"

"It just sounded like a good number."

Jim laughed and shook his head. "Sounded like a good number, eh?"

"Yeah," Mark said with an embarrassed grin. "I gave him reasons, too. I think he believed me. And I bet he'll go back to the Magician and try to sell him."

Jim wondered aloud if Ron was connected to the underworld and if he might be dangerous. "We'll try to check him out," he said.

"He wants to see some money from me," Mark said. "I've got to have cash to show him. Can you arrange that for tomorrow?"

"I'll try."

"Well, look, I can't let him call my bluff."
"I'll see what I can do."

Wednesday, 2 October

Jim returned this morning with four packets of "flash money" that appeared to contain a total of £2000 in £10 notes. "It's the best I could come up with," Jim said. Each stack of notes was sealed inside a cellophane envelope stamped by the Midland Bank. There were genuine £10 notes on the tops and bottoms, but in between were blank pieces of paper.

"Are you out of your damn mind?" Mark yelled. "I can't give him these! What if he grabs one and opens it up?"

"Don't let him."

"For God's sake, Jim, what kind of support is this? Why couldn't you get me some *real* money? I mean, the Bank of England still has a few extra quid, doesn't it?"

"But we can't give you cash. It's against the rules."

"That's terrific," Mark said with sarcasm. "This guy Ron is no dummy, you know. And Dave isn't either. They're gonna want to *count* these bills. If anybody should be suspicious of money, it's people involved with forgery. If I use these, I'm setting myself up to be exposed!"

When the doorbell rang at three o'clock, Mark handed the flash rolls to Jim and told him to take them upstairs.

The go-betweens entered with serious expressions. Ron's face, with its prominent cheekbones and protruding jaw, was covered with red blotches that betrayed his tension. He and Dave refused to take seats at the dining-room table. They stood there in challenging poses, waiting to see some cash.

Mark took the offense. "Have you talked to the Magician? Does he want my price or not?"

"He says the price is okay," Ron answered. "But he doesn't trust you."

"What the hell does that mean?"

"It means that we have shown good faith, but you 'aven't."

"Where's *your* good faith? Listen, this is the first time you've agreed to a deal! Until right now, you guys have been jerking me around!"

Ron's face twitched in anger. "How 'ave we done that?"

"Well, first Dave says he's the top man. I figured he was the guy who could make a decision. Then I'm told *you're* the boss. But both of you were lying! That's good faith?"

"We delivered samples to you," Ron argued. "Now it's your turn to show us something."

"Okay. Why don't you sit down?"

With an attitude of skepticism and hostility, Ron took a seat at the table. Dave followed, sitting across from him.

"I'll be right back," Mark said.

In the upstairs study, he asked Jim for the four cellophane envelopes and whispered, "Here we go," taking them and heading back down. He thought to himself that if Ron and Dave did discover that the envelopes contained flash money instead of the real thing, he could tell them, "Look, I didn't know who you guys were. You might have been rip-off artists. I didn't want to lose two thousand pounds in cash." Maybe that would be a believable excuse.

He tossed the packages on the dining-room table and said, "*Here* is the color of my money." At the same time, he was struck by a new idea. Inside one of the corner-wall cabinets was a shiny, three-ounce gold bar, from a Swiss bank, that he often took with him on his travels to foreign countries. It was a mere token, and represented all the gold that he owned, but perhaps it would divert their attention from the flash rolls.

Just as Ron and Dave were about to inspect what they thought were £2000 in sealed bank envelopes, Mark blurted out, "And I have something else that I'd like to show you." He grabbed the gold bar from the cabinet and swiftly placed it on top of the packages of nonexistent £10 notes.

The two counterfeiters were instantly distracted. Lifting up the gold bar, Ron said, "Is it hot?"

"No, it's clean. But I don't want to show any official transactions with it."

Ron fondled the bar as Dave looked on. "I'll show it to the Magician and see if it's acceptable," he said, forgetting about the fake paper money.

"That gold is worth about three hundred pounds," Mark said with relief as he pocketed the flash rolls. "Just tell him that's *also* the color of my dough. And," he added with bravado, "there's plenty more where that came from."

When Jim heard about the gold-bar maneuver, he swallowed hard and picked up the phone to call Superintendent Miller. He reported that Mark had used the flash money with success, but added, "I have something else to tell you, sir."

"Yes?"

"Yarry's given them a gold bar."

"A what?"

"Gold bar, sir."

"You let him part with his own money?"

"It was a spontaneous thing, sir."

"In other words, damn it all, you can't control him!"

"He's been ad-libbing the situation, sir, but I think he's doing what's required to build up a confidence level. And—"

"Goldie, you're dealing with an American citizen who is involved in a major operation being conducted by Scotland Yard! And you tell me this man glibly parts with a gold bar, without any previous instruction?"

"Yes, sir, but—"

"Well, it's obvious you can't control him. He's running off and conducting an operation of his own! Goldie, all you've got so far is a handful of forged notes. Five pieces of paper! How do we know the blokes will come back? You might never see them again! And if they *do* run off with that gold bar, we'll have a cranky American screaming his bloody head off! He'll say, 'Look, I was helping the Yard and now I've been robbed!' It could be a disaster, Jim."

"They're due to return tomorrow."

"Let's hope they bring that gold bar with them. Meanwhile, we desperately need to get a man in there to carry on in Yarry's place. He's got to be removed as soon as possible, understand? Because it's clear he's uncontrollable."

"Sir, I feel we're making progress over here. I think if we can keep it going, we'll get to the forger."

"Right now you worry about the gold bar!"

Stung by Superintendent Miller's anger, Jim realized that sooner or later he would have to stop being a buffer between Mark and the Yard, and take sides. During his eight-year career with the Metropolitan Police, he had been a by-the-book officer, adhering punctiliously to the rules. But this situation was totally unorthodox, requiring him to make judgments for which there were no official guidelines. For a week, Jim had been the invisible partner, hiding upstairs and relying solely on what Mark was reporting to him. The element of trust was vital.

He intuitively believed that Yarry could handle himself in tough situations and sensed that he was blessed with an unusual degree of flexibility. The gold-bar tactic might have been a procedural transgression, but it was also a stroke of brilliance. Perhaps it was typical of Yarry's character. The Yard had presented him with the problem of the flash rolls, and he had dealt with it instinctively and in his own way.

Jim did not reveal Miller's attitude to Mark, but instead gave him encouragement and even added, "The Yard is behind you one hundred percent."

Thursday,
3 October

When the go-betweens failed to appear on schedule, Jim Goldie began to fear that Superintendent Miller's skepticism had been justified. Meanwhile, Mark gave his assurance that he had no intention of complaining, in public or otherwise, about the loss of his gold bar. Perhaps the Yard would reimburse him, but that wasn't important. The collapse of the operation, which had been going on for nine days, would be a much greater blow. Both Jim and Mark were on the verge of admitting failure when, two hours late, Ron and Dave came to the door.

As the housekeeper served coffee in the dining room ("All I'm doing is feeding coffee to counterfeit-money dealers," Mark had joked), Ron reached into his jacket pocket and pulled out the gold bar. Mark concealed his elation, acting totally unconcerned.

"The Magician won't accept this," Ron said as he placed the gold bar on the table. "He wants full payment in English currency."

"Fair enough," Mark said. "But let's agree on a firm date for the transaction, okay?"

"You'll have to meet with the Magician."

"Fine. I'll need a few days to put together the amount of cash you want. I was hoping to do the deal *all* in gold, but cash is okay. I just need a little more time. But call your man right now and we'll set a date."

"I can't ring him for about an hour," Ron said.

"Then let's just wait," Mark replied. "Have some more coffee."

Now, he thought, what am I supposed to talk about with a pair of crooks for the next hour? It occurred to him that Ron and Dave would be impressed if he gave them the idea that he was part of some large criminal syndicate based in the States. Instead of being employed by an optical-import firm, why not by the Mafia?

"All this furniture," he said, "all through the house—it was given to me as a present."

Ron and Dave looked at him. At last Dave said, "I *knew* you was all right for the ready."

"Pardon?"

"Cash, you know."

"Well, my business partners are almost relatives. They're *family* associates," Mark said pointedly. "Do you understand?" Ron and Dave were silent, so he added totally on impulse, "In fact, they just sent me a new camera. It's a Polaroid SX.70."

"It has gadgets?" Ron asked, as if trying to sound knowledgeable.

"The latest model," Mark said. "It's just gone on sale in the U.K. Would you like to see it?"

"Sure," Ron said.

Mark went upstairs to fetch the camera, although he wasn't even sure what he might do with it. Anything to keep improvising, he thought. In the study, he grabbed it from the shelf and whispered to Jim, "They brought back the gold bar!" The detective's face brightened and he raised his thumb in the air. Mark also whispered that Ron was going to call the forger in less than an hour.

On his way downstairs, Mark's mind raced ahead to figure out how he might use the camera to his advantage. He had bought it in August, when he had flown from France to the United States for talks with the optical company's executives about the move to London. He wondered if he could find a way to take photographs of the counterfeiters for the police—unaware that C-11 had already done so.

"I'm expecting a whole shipment of these cameras," he told them when he returned to the dining room. Still improvising, he suddenly mentioned that he would be receiving "five hundred cameras as partial payment of a debt."

Ron looked skeptical. "Five hundred?"

"My organization in the States owes me a ton of money for a deal I did last spring. So they're sending me a shipment of cameras. Would you be interested in that kind of merchandise?"

"Is it hot?"

"Of course not," Mark said. "The organization is much too careful. Maybe you know someone who could take 'em off my hands."

"Maybe," Ron said, staring at him. "Where is the organization based?"

"New York and Florida, mainly. But it's also a worldwide operation, if you get my drift. For example, in *our* deal I'm using one of my men in Germany. He'll supply the cash."

"Is he English? American?"

"A German national," Mark improvised again, marveling at the fact that even he didn't know what he might say next.

"Maybe we could do business together," Ron said. "I happen to know of some opportunities."

"I'm always interested in something of good quality," Mark replied. "Do you have anything specific in mind?"

"Well, I'm expecting a consignment of diamonds, through a contact at the airport."

"What's the value?"

"About a hundred and fifty thousand pounds," Ron said. "Do you know a buyer?"

"Maybe I'd like to buy them," Mark replied, now thoroughly believing in his own performance. "Let me know when you have something tangible. My people can check it out for me."

The conversation drifted back to Mark's Polaroid SX.70 camera, which both Ron and Dave had been inspecting with curiosity. Again without any specific plan, Mark took the camera, aimed it at Dave and clicked the shutter.

Ron got to his feet in a rage. "What'd you do that for?"

"I want to show you how it works," Mark said. He handed the picture to Dave. Despite the growing tension in the room, he swung the camera around to Ron and clicked it again.

"Hey!" Ron yelled, reacting as if he'd been shot by a gun. "What the fuck's the matter with you?"

Mark took out the developed photograph and held it up. "Perfect," he said.

"You destroy that! Go on! Tear it up!"

"Take it easy," Mark said, but Ron was already moving around the table to get to him. He snatched the picture, still glaring at Mark, and tore it to shreds. Realizing that the incident had almost been disastrous, Mark turned their attention back to the counterfeit-money deal, talking rapidly about his desire for "one large transaction only."

When the hour had passed, Ron went to the phone in the hallway off the dining room. He dialed a number and said, "Is that you, Brad? . . . Brad, the American wants a firm date to do the deal. Can we—"

"Let me talk to him," Mark interrupted.

Ron put his hand up for Mark to stay away. "I'll ring you back in a minute," he said into the phone, quickly hanging up and turning to Mark. "What the hell's the matter with you? Nobody talks to him but me! Is that understood?" He picked up the phone and dialed again. "Brad? . . . That's right, the basic exchange as we discussed it . . . Right . . . He wants it done in one transaction."

"Or else there's no deal at all," Mark interrupted.

Ron glared at him in a fury, then turned back to the phone. "It's the only way he'll do it. . . . Okay. . . . Righto." He hung up and said to Mark, "Well, that's it. He's the top man."

"So what'd he say?"

"He agreed to be in contact with me tonight. I'll come back tomorrow at noon and we can make arrangements for the transfer."

"And we'll set a date for it to happen?"

"That's right."

"The man you just spoke to—was that the Magician?"

"That was him."

Jim reported to Scotland Yard that a meeting between Mark and the Magician, whose first name apparently was Brad, could be imminent. Ron was due back at the house the next day with word of how the transfer of money for £100,000 face value of forged notes was to be handled. Jim's superiors at the Yard expressed doubt that the forger himself would come out of hiding. If not, Mark would have to lure him out by demanding that the forger meet with his "money supplier," the so-called German national, who would have to be a German-speaking undercover agent from the Yard.

Friday,
4 October

When Mark answered the door at noon, he was bewildered to see Dave standing there alone. "Where's Ron?" he asked as they entered the dining room.

Dave turned to face him. "Look, the man only wants to do it in small deals. He doesn't like doing big deals. Too dangerous, he says. But he's willing to give you credit up front."

"What are you talking about?"

"The Magician has a policy of moving no more than a thousand notes at a time. He's been doing very well with that. So he's only going to give you a thousand notes to start with—a face value of five thousand pounds—on credit. You don't have to pay until after you've disposed of it. Then you receive the next shipment, and so on, for as many deals as you like. But only one parcel at a time."

Mark's spirits dropped. The Magician obviously had worked out a foolproof system enabling him to stay far removed from the action. If he never showed his face, it would be impossible to arrest him on conspiracy charges, much less for possession of counterfeit money. To get him for the actual printing of forged notes, requiring the confiscation of his negatives or plates, was even a more remote possibility. The only way to lure him, it seemed, was to appeal to his greed by offering one large sum of money for a single shipment. Yet even with the prospect of making a fast £30,000, he wouldn't budge. Apparently, the Magician knew the danger of greed and had taken steps to insulate himself from it. By permitting only "small" deals, he would never face a temptation to come into the open. There would be no way to persuade him to meet with any fake-money supplier from Germany. For Mark, it was as if a mental chess game had begun, with the Magician way ahead in the opening moves.

Turning on Dave in anger, he forced himself to believe more thoroughly than ever in his role as a member of the criminal world. "What's all this nonsense about?" he yelled. "We make a deal, we've been talking about it for over a week—now the man is trying to back down! I'm getting very annoyed!"

Dave seemed to sense that he was suddenly over his head in the situation. In an apologetic tone he said, "Listen, I've never met the Magician myself. I don't even know his name. All I'm doing is relaying Ron's message."

"Then you go find Ron and bring him here. If I *don't* see him soon, there's going to be trouble!"

"I don't know if I can make contact with him," said Dave, who was now visibly upset.

"Look, you find him!"

"I'll do my best."

"You had *better* do your best," Mark warned. But a new idea came to him and he added, "Wait here one second. Just sit down, Dave."

He hurried out of the room and upstairs. There was hardly time for prior consultation with Jim about what he was going to do. In the study, he said, "Look, Jim, I want you to come down and meet Dave. You're my brother-in-law. I want him to see you. Just give me a few minutes and then come on down." Jim grabbed the black leather jacket he had brought along for just such an occasion, although he hadn't expected it to happen so soon.

Mark rushed back downstairs. "Okay," he told Dave, his

tone becoming angrier by the moment, "if you can't find Ron, I'll have to send somebody to get him."

"I'll *try* to find him," Dave said.

"That's not good enough!"

Jim appeared in the doorway, wearing his leather jacket and looking every bit the part of a loyal soldier in some criminal gang. After the first glance at him, Dave could only believe that he was staring up at a muscle man.

"Are you all right, Mark?"

"Yes, come on in. Dave, meet Jim, my brother-in-law." The two men shook hands, Jim staring sullenly into Dave's eyes before moving around the table to a seat near the window. "Jim is a member of my organization," Mark went on. "He's my bodyguard." In the silence, Dave sat completely still as if waiting to see what might happen next. "Jim is responsible for the safety of my household and my interests," Mark said as he glared at Dave. "You've seen that I keep money in the house, and gold—you didn't think I was stupid enough not to be protected, did you?"

"No," Dave said in a near whisper.

Mark turned to Jim. "He tells me that he can't find Ron."

Dave said, "It's true! I don't know where he is. He's dropped me right in it."

"Doesn't he want to do the deal?" Jim asked.

"I don't know what's going on," Dave said in a plea for understanding. "This is too much for me now."

"Just find Ron or I'll send Jim out to get him."

"I'll do my best."

"Good-bye," Mark snapped.

Dave returned with Ron in less than fifteen minutes. The cockney was in an aggravated, belligerent mood. He was swaggering across Wilton Place with clenched fists at his sides. Mark stood in the doorway and Ron, striding up to him, said, "Did you threaten my man here?"

"Come in," Mark shot back, starting upstairs.

"Nobody threatens my people! You'd better know that!"

As if on cue, Jim appeared at the landing. "Mark, you having a problem?"

"You his minder?" Ron asked as he stared up at him.

"I see after Mark's interests," Jim said evenly. "He doesn't like looking behind himself, so I do it for him."

When they had climbed up to the study, Mark remembered that he had draped a shoulder-holster over the coat hook the night before. As a teenager, he had befriended a New York City policeman who, some years later, sent him the holster as a birthday gift. Mark did not own a gun, but he had brought out the holster and put it on display precisely so the two men would think he did. Now, as he had planned, he grabbed it off the coat hook, as if trying to conceal it, and crammed it into a desk drawer. The swift but deliberately awkward gesture caught the attention of both Ron and Dave, who stared at the drawer in silence.

After about five minutes of small talk, Mark ordered that the meeting be moved back downstairs, adding, "Jim, I don't think I'll need you for this. Wait up here."

"Okay," said Jim, who by now was resigned to the fact that he never knew what Mark would say or do next.

In the dining room, Ron insisted, "We do deals *our* way! If you don't like it, that's too damn bad!"

"I *don't* like the way you do deals."

"Then don't do them at all!"

In the midst of the argument, Monica appeared with coffee. A cheerful British woman with long blond hair and a relaxed manner, she greeted the men in a polite tone and unintentionally defused Ron's anger.

"Thank you," he said as she poured his coffee. "Thank you indeed, ma'am."

When Monica left the room, Mark addressed Ron in a calm but firm tone of voice, taking control of the debate. "Look, once you make a deal with me, you make a deal. It's done. There's no backing out. It's too late. I really don't care what your man wants. He's committed to doing a deal with me and it's going to be done. I'm not accepting any five-thousand-pound drabs."

"That's your problem, then."

"All these meetings—every time you walk into this house you're exposing *me* to risk. This is my home! My wife and kids live here! And why the hell do *you* want to keep exposing yourself to so much risk?"

"We can do the transactions somewhere else, then."

"I'm talking about accomplishing everything in one lump! Why take *twenty times* the necessary risk? It just doesn't make good sense to me."

Ron took a sip of his coffee. In the silence, his attitude seemed to change. "Mark, I'd like to do it in one deal, but the Magician wants it done his way."

"Well, it's not 'on' his way. I won't do it, and neither should you. We can't do these little deals. It's not safe for me, it's not safe for you. We'll do it *our* way, because it's safe for *all* of us, not just for your boss. I'm concerned for our mutual safety—not only mine, but yours."

"I appreciate that," Ron admitted.

"So go back and tell your man that we'll do the deal in one lump or not at all," Mark said, and as Ron and Dave were leaving, he pressed his advantage. "You might also tell this Magician that *I* seem to be more concerned about protecting you than *he* is." Ron nodded and they shook hands. "If you worked for me," Mark went on, "I'd make *sure* you didn't go through all this hassle for a quid."

"Thanks, Mark," Ron said in a sudden show of intimacy. "Maybe I *should* be working for you," he added with a laugh.

"Just get in touch with me as soon as you can."

Friday, 4 October– Sunday, 6 October

There was no doubt in Mark's mind that he had deflected Ron's antagonism away from himself and toward the forger. The quick-tempered cockney was now a fledgling ally, working to persuade the printer to go along with one large transaction. The question was whether he would be forceful enough.

The remainder of Friday passed, then all of Saturday. At nine o'clock on Sunday evening, Ron called from a public phone to say that he still had been unable to "reach the man."

"Is anything wrong?" Mark asked.

"I think he's out of town. But I just wanted to let you know I'm trying. I'll get back to you as soon as I talk to him."

It was time to withdraw the pressure and lie back. The tension could grow too quickly, causing the fragile relationship to collapse. "Okay," Mark said in a subdued tone. "When he comes back to town, call me and we'll sit down and talk about it again. All I want to do is get it over with and make some money."

"Same here, Mark. I *want* to see the deal done."

"It's up to your man. If you can make him see the light, let me know."

Monday,
7 October

Jim arrived in the morning and the waiting began. The two men had breakfast and sat around talking for the rest of the morning. At lunchtime they walked over to the Turks Head pub on nearby Motcomb Street. They left instructions for the housekeeper to take any messages, but there were none.

The waiting went on through the afternoon. Jim spent some time in the early evening with Mark's daughters, Samantha and Melissa, bouncing them on his knees and singing Scottish nursery rhymes, much to their delight.

At dinner, Jim said, "Mark, you're like the spider trying to entice the fly. The Magician has been told that you've got this big criminal organization. You're sitting here in a beautiful, expensive house in Knightsbridge, a man of means, and you're offering him the biggest single deal he could imagine. He's probably never unloaded more than a thousand notes at a time, and you're talking about twenty thousand. That's an enticing web."

"Maybe so," Mark said, "but I don't think he cares about that. I have the feeling he's just not greedy enough."

"I can't believe he'll walk away completely."

"Well, we've done all we can."

Tuesday, 8 October–
Thursday, 10 October

Jim returned for more of the same speculation on Tuesday
and Wednesday. On Thursday morning, Superintendent
Miller told Jim by phone that Operation Wellington was
being canceled.

"We can't have an officer sitting over there doing nothing. You'd better come back here and help us develop
some more leads. The D.5/2 notes are coming into circulation even faster, now. We've got to crack this case before
we have a panic on our hands."

"Let me hang in until the week is out," Jim pleaded.

"In our professional judgment, you're in a losing cause."

"Just until the end of tomorrow. If nothing happens, I'll
forget it."

"If you like, Jim. But you'd better accept the fact it's
over."

The D.5/2 investigation had already become the largest
and most intense counterfeiting case in Scotland Yard's
history. The situation amounted to a growing, but silent,
national crisis. So far the currency had been inflated with
an untold number of forged £5 notes, yet the public was
still unaware. When would it end? In their worst night-
mares, officials of the Bank of England could envision the
Magician going on month after month, year after year,
perhaps producing £10 and £20 notes as well.

The Bank of England's chief concern was the quality of
the forged bills, but the Yard was even more frustrated
by the forger's distribution system. Detectives had come

to the conclusion that the Magician was sitting securely at the top of a pyramid of distributors, happily printing his money while dealing only with a small group of contacts. The notes were being transferred to other middlemen who took the risk of finding potential buyers. The pyramid continued downward and outward, through a series of sales, to the street-level passers, who were exposed to the greatest danger of all—although, because of the bills' excellent quality, the "utterers" were having no trouble in purchasing goods and services at full face value.

All previously known or suspected forgers were still under heavy surveillance. A few taverns in London were being watched closely, because they were frequented by people who had dealt with counterfeit money in past years. Again, however, there were no solid leads. Large quantities of the forged £5 notes had been traced back to the Catford Dog Track in southeast London and detectives hoped to catch a passer, but no arrests had been made.

Meanwhile, Operation Wellington continued in Knightsbridge under the direction of Detective Constable Goldie and, by now, that particular phase of the investigation had become something of a joke. Who was this American trying to tell the Yard what to do? All Goldie had, so far, was a grand total of five samples. A cockney named "Ron" was bragging about having contact with the Magician, but now he had backed away and Jim Goldie was sitting there with nothing to show for his trouble. He was allowing the impetuous Yank to manipulate him with persuasive talk and big dreams of accomplishing what all of Scotland Yard could not. Well, Goldie was inexperienced and would have to learn the hard way.

Mark and Jim continued to offer each other encouragement. They needed to keep talking, not only to buttress their spirits but also to block out the overwhelming silence of the telephone. Jim was now in the house up to eighteen hours a day, arriving early each morning. He and Mark would eat all their meals together and continue talking late into the night, when Jim would return home to his wife and two children, at their modest home in New Malden, to catch some sleep and change clothes.

"I really wanted to see it through to the end," Mark said. "I'm sorry it worked out this way."

"He still might call," Jim mused, knowing that on Monday he would have to return to the forgery squad and join the rest of the counterfeiting investigation.

Mark set up some business appointments for the following week, but he had little enthusiasm for going off on another marathon of sales meetings with optical-company executives.

"Hey," he joked, "maybe I'll get Dave as a driver again."

"The odds against that are too incredible to think about," Jim replied. "You walk out the door and of all the cabs in London, you get *that* one. It was phenomenal the *first* time around."

They were becoming fast friends. Their unusual partnership had led to an openness that was rare for both of them. Spending all that time together, they talked more candidly and at greater length than either man had ever done with his closest friends, while they also marveled at how different they were. They were the same age, but in virtually every other respect they might have come from separate planets.

Jim had been raised in a small village of Scotland, dreaming all during his childhood of becoming a professional athlete. He left school at age fifteen to work with his father, a bricklayer, and within two years he was signed to a first-division soccer team in England—the equivalent of becoming part of the National Football League in the United States directly after high school. But star status was elusive, and Jim slipped to second- and third-division teams because he lacked consistency as a player. By the age of twenty-six, his career was over.

When London's Metropolitan Police received his application for employment, he was welcomed with open arms. Here was a tall, handsome, strapping athlete who, from a public-relations point of view, would be a great asset. Commissioner John Waldron himself was determined to transform the Metropolitan Police football club into a worthy competitor in the Metropolitan League, whose other squads were made up of second-stringers from professional teams. Goldie could become a leading soccer player for the cops and a coach as well. It would be a way of continuing with the sport he loved while developing a new career.

After basic training, Jim was sent to Wimbledon, where he patrolled as a rookie in uniform for seventeen months. He applied for the Criminal Investigation Department and spent the next year and a half as a probationary detective constable in plainclothes. He was confirmed as a CID member and transferred to Tooting, a predominantly black area, where he developed a reputation for being sympathetic toward those he questioned or arrested. From there he was sent to Scotland Yard, headquarters of London's Metropolitan Police and "home" for at least a thousand city detectives. Jim continued as one of the top players on the police football team, taking time off for training and traveling to games; but the leg injury soon put an end to that phase of his career.

Everything in his life had been solid and stable. A popular youngster in high school, he had married his sweetheart from teenage years, when he was twenty-three. Now they had a son, John, and a daughter who, like one of Mark's girls, was named Samantha. Jim and his wife, Linda, were grateful for having a small suburban house and his secure income as well as her paycheck from secretarial work.

Jim did not share the "police mentality" that so many of his colleagues seemed to have and, because of his athletic career, he was friendly with top-ranking officers at the Yard and even on close terms with Superintendent Miller's governor, Commander Harold Grant. Jim had yet to go over Miller's head for any support in the current case, which was certainly his most important opportunity so far as a detective. He had the urge to ring up Commander Grant and express his feeling that he and Mark were on the right track, but if the go-betweens did not call or return in person, there was little point in doing so. In addition, he wanted to avoid alienating Miller.

He could only speculate, along with Mark, about Ron's attempts to persuade the forger, who seemed so mysteriously reluctant to make a quick, huge profit. How could he resist the temptation? Who was this man called the Magician? For that matter, Jim thought, what sort of man is this American in whom I'm investing so much trust and hope? Who is Mark Yarry?

"I left home at seventeen," Mark said, adding that he had lived in a low-income neighborhood in Queens, New York. The family was in an apartment above the old Hobart Theatre. The only advantage, to Mark, was that he could get into the movies without paying. The fantasies on the screen were free.

The home was enveloped by an artistic, musical, and highly literate atmosphere. Mark's mother was a violinist and his younger sister aspired to become a professional dancer. His father, a dentist who treated his patients in the apartment, was a studious man to whom books were sacred. Mark and his sister were expected to read everything—magazines, periodicals, biographies, and novels and, of course, *The New York Times.*

"You had to read it and understand it, because you were questioned about it at the dinner table. Really tough questioning. It was expected that you comprehended basic, fundamental laws of economics and political theory. If you said something that sounded stupid, my father would say, 'What do you mean by that?' or 'You don't know what you're talking about, do you?' It was that kind of environment."

His parents had many friends with a variety of points of view, but the Yarry household was definitely left wing in outlook. The Communist-backed *Daily Worker* would arrive in a brown paper bag and the "underdog" was always championed.

"My father was truly, in the finest sense, a socialist. He still is. He believed in socialized medicine and other causes when they were in no way fashionable. He was absolutely dedicated to helping people. More patients used to walk *out* of his office with money than came in with it."

On the other hand, Mark's mother longed to move to Manhattan to be closer to the museums and galleries. She filled the apartment with Chinese porcelain, silk rugs, paintings, and the like. Mark and his sister went with her almost every Sunday to the Metropolitan Museum or the Museum of Modern Art.

"I only began to appreciate it at a later age, because there was so much peer pressure outside the home. The kids playing baseball or football wouldn't accept me because they knew I came from a different economic background. I was the 'rich kid' to them. Their fathers were laborers or mechanics or factory hands who worked hard, physically, for their money. And here I was, the dentist's son who dressed a little better, who went to camp in the summer, who could do things. So I was not accepted and there wasn't anything I could do about it."

Jim Goldie had never been to New York City, much less to the Borough of Queens, but he tried to imagine the setting. What intrigued him most was the gradual coming together of the puzzle that was Mark Yarry, debonair businessman. The FBI check on him was favorable, but it shed no light on his character. What sort of man moves to London and, during his very first day on a new job, tells a counterfeit-money supplier that he might be interested in buying some? What sort of man forgets all about his work and jumps with both feet into the roles of criminal and police agent? It was almost easier for Jim to imagine the Magician than to comprehend the man in whose house he was spending so much time.

At an early age, Mark felt he had become qualified —solely through self-education—to be a doctor.

"In our home there were hundreds of medical books covering anatomy, psychiatry, surgery, pediatrics, obstetrics—you name it and it was there. After reading everything else in the apartment, I started on those. I had an extremely retentive memory—in fact, to this day I can recite the symptoms of many diseases and the required treatment. I was twelve. I just started at A and went through to Z. After I did it once, I went through each topic three times. I learned the *Merck Manual* and *Gray's Anatomy* almost by heart and went through specialized books on diagnosis, radiology, and so forth."

Soon he could sit down with his father's physician

friends and converse with them in depth. In time, Mark's father grew more comfortable with his son's physical examinations than with those of his own doctor. Later, in California, Mark tried to take the State Medical Boards, despite the fact that he had gone neither to college nor to medical school. He simply felt that if he could pass the tests, he should be allowed to practice medicine in the state. But there was no room in the bureaucracy for that.

"Once I came across an accident on the New Jersey Turnpike. Three people were horribly injured—the bleeding was acute—and I feel that without the kind of first-aid attention I gave them, they would have died."

It occurred to Jim that Mark's confidence in his ability as a "doctor" was similar to his self-assurance as a "white-collar criminal" and a "police undercover agent" in the current situation. It was as if he became involved in these roles so thoroughly that while "onstage" he blocked out everything else in life. He made good use of his retentive memory, drawing on bits and pieces of information in order to be convincing. He had in-depth knowledge of an astonishing number of topics. He had the intensity of a "method" actor, but in real-life dramas. Perhaps there were two Magicians.

Mark's formal education was limited. He had gone to public school in Queens, within walking distance of home. Right after high school, he forged a birth certificate in order to join the Army. *Forged,* Jim thought with a smile.

"I went into a Reserve program for six months of active duty. I seriously considered making a career in the military, because it was something to identify with. You could be one of the boys, part of the crowd. There was a sense of belonging to something and being comfortable with your contemporaries. I also did a tour in the Air Force and that was enjoyable, too. I'd always been in love with flying.

"We lived within a stone's throw of La Guardia Airport. When I was eight or nine, I'd take my bicycle over there to look at the airplanes. At eleven, I got up enough courage to go into the airport itself and ask the maintenance people if I could go on board when the planes were on the ground. I wanted to see what it was like. And they let me sit in the cockpits."

At thirteen, he went to the local Flushing Airport and met a man who owned and operated a flying school. They made an arrangement whereby Mark received flying lessons in exchange for logging in the pilots and students, collecting the money, and selling soda pop. He went there twice a week after school and all day on Saturdays. He learned to fly.

"You had to be seventeen to hold a private pilot's license, but at fourteen I was zooming around the skies in the busiest traffic zone in the States. I got my student-pilot's license when I was sixteen and proceeded to fly aircraft considerably more sophisticated than any license permitted. For me, flying has been a form of escape."

Another form might have been his piano playing in plush hotel bars and nightclubs in New York. His real love was the old stuff, tunes from the twenties, thirties, and forties. Play it again, Mark. Something to identify with. A way of belonging somewhere. And yet, Jim thought, the piano playing was also something for which he was not "qualified" in the usual sense. Mark seemed to "escape" precisely so he would face the task of being an "outsider" who must earn acceptance with each new role.

Until he was twenty-five, he went through long periods of frustration and uncertainty about his direction in life. He worked at an advertising firm, took a job in a mail-order house, became a travel agent. Just before his marriage in 1966, he flew for an airline based in Frankfurt, Germany. Monica, working for Pan Am, had been born in

Yorkshire and raised in the Bristol area of England. They moved to Rome.

"I started my own company in Italy. It was created to steal engineers and professionals from Europe and send them on the happy 'brain train' to the United States. The United States was terribly short of engineers in the 1960s, so we recruited Italians, Frenchmen, and Germans, acting as a quasi-employment agency. It was very successful, but after six months the Italian police closed us down because, under the law, only the government was supposed to run an employment agency in Italy. We weren't *really* an employment office, but they construed us as such."

Against the rules. Outside the system. Time to move on.

"We left Rome and moved to New York City. I'd always had an interest in the publishing business, so I looked for a job in that field."

He wound up with an advertising firm, selling space for *The Financial Times* of London, the *Far Eastern Economic Review*, *Newsweek International*, and a professional magazine called the *Financial Analyst's Journal*, among other publications. And did so well that *The Financial Times* invited him to London for a visit.

"When I arrived, I told the *Times* people what I thought was wrong with their publication and they had me taken off the account. How dare *I* tell *them* how to change their format?"

Well, Jim thought, the same way you dare believe that you can crack this counterfeiting case all by yourself.

"A fellow in New York named Gilbert Kaplan was interested in starting a new magazine and he called me. I was twenty-six, he was twenty-five. I went around with a dummy issue and sold space. It became the most successful magazine in the financial field—*Institutional Investor*. We had a circulation of only twenty-five thousand, but those subscribers included some of the most important people in the world. We had outrageous advertising rates. It became a public company in 1969 and I made a lot of money. I held a fair amount of stock and sold all of it. After being with the magazine for five years, I decided it was time for a change."

"Time to move on?"

"Right. So I told Kaplan I was going to Europe and take it easy for a couple of years, to think over what I wanted to do next."

He moved Monica and the girls from their New York penthouse over to a beautiful estate in Surrey, England. By April 1971, at the age of thirty-one, Mark Yarry was in retirement. And, Jim thought, temporarily burned out.

The puzzle picture grew clearer. There was, Jim felt, a pattern. Mark tended to throw himself into a pursuit for a period of time, with great intensity, and then withdraw to recuperate. It hardly came as a surprise to learn about Mark's ballooning escapades. Here again, almost solely on impulse, he had taken up a new skill and mastered it, only to retreat until it was time for some other challenge.

"I was sitting at home in Surrey, just relaxing, when I happened to watch a show on the BBC about ballooning. It was a fabulous scene in the wintertime, and here were those colorful, huge objects flying around the sky. And the balloonists were breaking open bottles of champagne and having picnic lunches while they flew! The whole thing was out of a nineteenth-century novel."

He placed a call to Donald Cameron, the balloonist who had been featured on the television program, and introduced himself as an American who would "love to have a ride." A week later, Mark was lifting off from a football field in Wales. After a thrilling flight, he ordered a balloon specially built for him. Cameron taught him how to operate it.

Before long, Mark was playing host on Sunday mornings at his estate, offering a beautiful setting for his new-found ballooning friends to have flying parties. He provided them with drinks and food and created an almost dream-like world in his own backyard. Here was romance, adventure, and acceptance. He was one of them, a fellow balloonist. In short order he had that in-depth knowledge of the subject. He and Cameron went on to set the world-duration record and, in 1972, they made the first hot-air Alps crossing, which *Life* magazine captured in a two-page photograph.

Mark's interest in philately was kindled during the same "retirement" period. "My father is a serious philatelist, but I'd never had the desire to collect stamps. Maybe the Old World charm of my environment in Surrey was what sparked it. I became interested in postal history, which was my father's specialty, and made some original discoveries." He wrote articles on philately and developed a highly specialized collection of experimental cancellations from the mid-nineteenth century. Mark also joined the Royal Philatelic Society, of which his father had been a member for many years. He developed an interest in forgeries.

"I was really enjoying life. In the financial community in New York, I'd often felt like a social worker for the rich. To me, worrying about the buck is not what life is all about. But you get into the game, where each player is judged by the number of chips he has, and there's pressure to conform to that value system."

If you want acceptance in a certain world, you play its game. You drive a Mercedes, stay at the finest hotels, and eat in the best restaurants. You buy jewelry and furs and provide nannies and housekeepers, all the trappings. In London, Mark was a member of the Clermont, Curzon, and Playboy clubs, which he had joined before moving to

France, to the Villa Cinderella with its swimming pool and nearby casinos, discotheques, and restaurants along the Riviera.

"I was just spending money. I've always loved the good life. I really think I was born two hundred years late. If I'd lived in the eighteenth century, I probably would have been considered a gentlemanly rogue. I would have been much happier in that kind of society."

Once settled in the south of France, Mark began to look for a new business challenge. He flew to New York to see an old friend who owned a successful optical-import company. One topic of discussion was the potential for importing eyeglass frames into the Common Market. Back in France, he received a letter saying that it might be sensible to set up a European headquarters in England. Faced with the prospect of asking Monica to move back after only eight months, he arranged for the house in Knightsbridge as an enticement.

"We left Cannes with the two kids and a pussycat and I drove the thousand miles back up here. It was a terrible trip. The cat got arrested by the British customs people, thrown into a box, and sent off to quarantine for six months. I had two flat tires. The girls were carsick. Monica and I got indigestion. By the time we got to London, we looked more like refugees than experienced travelers. It was really exhausting.

"We rested up and I made appointments for the week of September 23. My first day on the job was on that Tuesday morning. I went out the door, stuck my hand up, and Dave pulled his taxicab around."

If the Yard had tried to create an "agent in place," it never could have matched this setup. Mark's children were continuing their French education in London; Monica, no longer an airline hostess, went about her daily routine; and anyone watching the house could not suspect a trap in a million years.

Jim was fascinated as he listened to Mark talk about his travels in South America, Africa, Asia, Australia, New Zealand, and on and on, but he also felt strangely sad for him. It was as if Mark had no way of finding his true self. His "retirement" period had probably been meant to provide him with time to reflect and look inward, to locate that self, but it hadn't worked. Instead, he still looked outside, to challenges and adventures. He became a kind of mirror, shaping himself into a reflection of what other people wanted to see. Was it to gain their acceptance, the way he had tried unsuccessfully as a youngster to become one of the gang? You want me to read medical books? Okay, I'll read so much that I'll become as good as any doctor. Want me to be a pilot? A stamp collector? A balloonist? A piano player? A businessman? Okay—I'll shape myself into those images until I become them. If I'm expected to be a rich man, I'll not only make money but spend it better than anyone else, too. I'll tip the cabdrivers and doormen and waiters and become a reflection of *their* desires. You want me to be a wheeler-dealer who buys counterfeit money? Or an agent for Scotland Yard? Just keep watching the mirror until you see the perfect forgery of what you want.

Friday,
11 October

It was the end of the week and, for both Mark and Jim, the result was disappointment and depression. Perhaps they would go out for dinner with Monica and Linda, have a good time, relax, and try to forget it for a while. Partnership had led to friendship, so it wasn't a total loss. . . .

At six o'clock, the phone rang.

"Mark," came the cockney accent, "it's Ron. I want to arrange a meet between you and the man."

Mark held the phone away and made a silent scream of victory. Jim held his breath.

"Sure," Mark said into the phone.

"Where do you think we could do it?" Ron asked.

"Well, I don't want to meet here at the house anymore. How about the Carlton Tower Hotel around the corner?"

"All right, Mark. Eleven o'clock on Sunday morning?"

"Fine."

"I'll introduce you to the man. Your arrangement will be made at the highest level."

"See you there," Mark said.

When he had hung up, he and Jim Goldie whooped and hollered and grabbed each other's arms, jumping up and down like children. Apparently Ron had worked hard over the past days to convince the Magician to change his position. Ron had looked into the mirror that was Mark Yarry and, after all, had seen the reflection of his dreams.

It was no wonder that high Government officials were keeping pressure on the Yard to eliminate the source of the forged £5 notes. Britain was facing its worst economic crisis in twenty-five years, with high unemployment, an invidious trade balance, a devastated stock market, and a 17-percent rate of inflation. Any further weakening of public confidence in the currency would be ill-timed, to say the least.

Meanwhile, terrorist attacks were being stepped up. Explosions shattered two pubs in Guildford, Surrey, thirty miles southwest of London, killing three men and two women and injuring fifty-four other patrons. Bombs were going off in mailboxes, at Army bases, near national monuments—even at foreign embassies in Knightsbridge, not far from Wilton Place. On this Friday night, while Mark and Jim were celebrating the continuance of Operation Wellington, bombs exploded in two London military clubs, sending scores of men and women into the glass-strewn streets. So far, in 1974, more than two hundred bombs had turned up in Britain. The IRA's campaign to pressure the British Government into getting out of Northern Ireland showed no signs of a letup. If the flood of D.5/2 notes was part of that campaign, as yet there had been no confirmation from any IRA spokesman, nor did the Yard's three thousand detectives have any evidence.

Superintendent Miller of the forgery squad received word that Jim Goldie had called the Yard with a message. the go-betweens had made contact and a meeting between Mark and the Magician had been set. Miller called the house and questioned Jim about the wisdom of letting Mark go alone. "Once again," he said, "you've let the thing get out of your hands."

"I have to trust him," Jim replied.

"But why can't you go along, too?"

"I'm not sure I'd be accepted. I'm supposedly here to guard his house and family."

"All right," Miller growled, "but this is highly irregular and dangerous. Report to me as soon as Yarry returns."

Sunday, 13 October

"Gonna meet the great man himself," Mark said with a smile as he was leaving the house.

"Just be careful," Jim said.

Mark turned briefly on the sidewalk and the two men laughed. There was a bond.

As he walked down Wilton Place, it seemed to Mark as if this were the most important moment of his life. It was a bright, sunny morning, quite warm, and he found himself striding along with a tremendous surge of anticipation. Will the Magician really be there?

He passed Wilton Crescent and walked west on Motcomb Street, until he came to the Carlton Tower on Cadogan Place. Overlooking a tree-filled garden square bordered by handsome houses, the hotel was one of the most luxurious in all of London. Mark had stayed here many times before and had made sure, as he always did, to tip all the right people.

The doorman, in his light-gray tails and white gloves, acknowledged him with a tip of his top hat and a smile. "Good morning, Mr. Yarry."

"Lovely day," Mark replied, pleased to be remembered after an absence of nearly nine months.

The plush, white-marbled foyer was bustling with well-dressed guests and courteous, efficient porters. Mark strolled toward the news kiosk in search of Ron, who suddenly appeared outside the hotel's glass front wall and gestured for Mark to wait. He disappeared, but in a few seconds returned with another man. Both came through the revolving door into the lobby.

This new man, Mark noticed, had a more sophisticated appearance than either Dave or Ron. The man was dressed in a conservative suit and tie. He was perhaps forty, with brown hair, and his blue-gray eyes darted around as if he were taking in the entire scene at once. It must be the Magician, Mark thought as he made a motion for them to follow him up the stairs to the mezzanine. They got halfway up when the hotel's general manager, on his way down, brightened at the sight of Mark and held out his hand. "Ah, good morning, sir! Welcome back! Good to see you again!"

Mark stood there with the two counterfeit-money dealers waiting behind him. "Thank you," he said, shaking hands. He continued up to the mezzanine, relieved to be spared the awkwardness of having to introduce his companions to the manager; but there was little question that they had been impressed by the cordial reception.

They walked past the elegant Chelsea Room, a French restaurant decorated in oranges and browns, to the hotel's coffee lounge. The atmosphere was that of a living room, complete with cushioned chairs and sofas and large, square coffee tables. Mark led the two men to a table at the far end.

When they were seated, Ron said, "Mark, this is Brad," then leaned back as if to remove himself.

Mark and Brad shook hands, staring into each other's eyes. They were interrupted by a waitress who took their orders and Mark casually lit a cigarette. "We have a problem" he said. Brad nodded slightly, so he went on. "It has to do with these multiple transactions. Let me explain my point of view," Mark continued, outlining his objection to "small deals" because they would involve too much risk for everybody.

Brad replied in a quiet tone of voice, "You have a logical argument, Mark. But I'm afraid it's impossible to do this any other way."

"Can you tell me the reason?"

"I've had too much trouble with large transactions. The tension becomes too great. People react in unexpected ways. It requires more of my personal attention than I'd like. I'm going against my own rule by even having this meeting with you. If you had gone along with *my* way, we could have completed at least three or four transactions by now."

"How do I know you have the full amount that I want?"

Brad smiled at him as the waitress brought coffee and departed. "If you won't take *my* word, the only other knowledgeable source would be the Bank of England. And believe me, *they* know the amount exists."

"Maybe you haven't dealt with someone like me before," Mark said. "I have more resources than the people who've been buying your product. I'm offering thirty thousand pounds for a face value of one hundred thousand—clean and simple. Maybe *that's* the reason you're meeting with me. If you can break one rule, you can break another."

Brad shifted uneasily in his chair. "I've told you the way it is and that's that."

Mark kept staring at him. "You *are* the top man, aren't you?"

"Yes." .

"And you're willing to let this whole thing go down the drain? You'll just walk away from it?"

"That's right," Brad said evenly.

"So we're at a standoff."

Brad nodded, but with an expression on his face that was almost apologetic. "I suppose we are."

"Look," Mark said at last, "are you the man who can make this deal or aren't you?" He stared coldly into Brad's eyes again, this time with the most menacing look that he could muster.

Brad held his gaze on Mark. "I *am* the top distributor, but I have to talk to the printer."

Mark sat back in silence, unable to hide his disappointment. For the second time, he thought, I've been led up the mountain in a ruse. How many *more* middlemen are there?

"I'm sick of this runaround," he said, thinking that the Magician was much more clever than he had expected. Maybe *nobody* knew his real identity; maybe the forger passed along his shipments of counterfeit notes by some sort of courier system that allowed him to remain totally insulated. Brad could be receiving packages of notes without really knowing their source.

Brad said, "I've been instructed to tell you that all the printer is willing to let out of his control, at any one time, is a thousand notes. A face value of five thousand pounds. You can have the delivery on credit. After each shipment has been paid for, another thousand notes will be delivered immediately. There can be as many shipments as you like."

"I've heard all this before. You know my objections."

"I understand, but that's the only way the man will do a bloody deal."

"This is a complete waste of my time," Mark said. "It's a waste of *your* time, too."

As the two men debated back and forth, Mark was thinking that his entire involvement in the case could take much longer than he had expected. If he worked on gaining Brad's friendship, and on luring him into a fantasy of being able to make a huge deal, maybe there would be some progress. But the idea of wrapping up the case in a jiffy had been dispelled.

Brad continued to act in a low-key manner, but he was also forthright and open, at one point responding to Mark's reference to the danger by saying, "Look, if I get caught doing this, that's the way it is. That's the risk I take. I know I could go to jail, but I'm prepared to pay that price."

"Well," Mark said, "if you want *my* money, you'll have to go back to the printer and convince him that this deal has to be done as one lump. That's the bottom line."

"Would you settle for a compromise?"

"Like what?"

"The printer might agree to release as many as five thousand notes at one time. It would require only four deals instead of twenty."

Mark thought a moment. It seemed that Brad was trying to bridge the gap. Perhaps it was best to show some flexibility at this point. "You think that you can persuade him?"

"I might be able to."

"And deliver twenty-five thousand pounds to me on credit?"

"I think so. The man might go for it."

Encouraged, Mark said, "Well, I don't like it, but let me tell you something, Brad: I don't want any ifs, ands, or buts this time. Tell me right now if you can make the delivery. Yea or nay?"

"I'm almost positive, Mark."

"Almost isn't good enough."

"I think if he understands who you are, he'll—"

"You tell him I'm willing to compromise," Mark interrupted. "If I can, so can he."

"All right," Brad said.

"Do you have direct contact with the printer?"

"Yes," Brad replied evenly.

"How do I know you're not lying again?"

"I'm telling you, Mark, that I'll bring five thousand notes to you."

"Where and when?"

"We'll come by your place tomorrow at four-thirty and pick you up," Brad went on. "The delivery will take place in the back of a taxicab."

Ron became animated and said in a loud, excited whisper, "You see, Mark, that's the safest way!" He went on to explain that they liked to make "transfers" in cabs because the taxi regulations gave drivers twenty-four hours to take any "abandoned property" to a police station. If questioned, a driver caught with counterfeit money in his cab could feign surprise and claim it had been left behind by a previous fare.

"Very clever," Mark said. "By the way, I'd like my brother-in-law to come with me."

"Okay," Brad said, "but we also have to arrange for your payment to us later on. At one pound fifty per note, that's seventy-five hundred pounds."

Mark nodded, reasoning that surely the Yard would supply the sum, given the importance of keeping the operation going. When the negotiations ended, he suggested that Brad and Ron leave the hotel first. "I'll take care of the check," he added.

After they had gone, he sat there realizing how exhausted he was. At least there was some movement, although the Magician still might not allow himself to be tempted. The mysterious forger remained far removed from the action, at a distance that was both comfortable and safe.

Monday,
14 October

With word that £25,000 in forged notes would be delivered, Superintendent Miller dispatched one of his higher-ranking officers to act as a direct link between himself and Jim Goldie. He selected Detective Sergeant Edward Franklin, a six-feet-six, two hundred forty-pound bear of a man, and instructed him to "go get a feel for what's happening over there" and report back in person. Franklin arranged to meet with Mark and Jim at the Turks Head pub at noon.

The popular watering hole had a friendly, warm atmosphere, with patrons four-deep at the bar and seated at tables along one side and in the rear. Others stood by the wall, resting their mugs and plates on a counter. Mark and Jim had no trouble finding Sergeant Franklin, whose receding hairline rose high above the heads of the lunchtime crowd. He held up his beer mug and motioned for them to make their way over. "He's huge," Mark said as they jostled toward him.

"Franklin is tough," Jim said, "but he's really a pussycat. A terrific, lovable guy. Don't let his looks fool you—he's one of the sharpest men we have. And he knocks back beer like it's water."

When Jim made the introductions, Mark stuck his hand out and felt it swallowed up and squeezed into numbness by Franklin's giant paw. With a wide grin, his eyes seeming to bulge as he looked down, Edward Franklin said, "Well, well, well! So this is the bloody Yank that we can't control, eh?"

Mark could not help laughing. He felt an instant rapport with this plainclothes sergeant who had been nicknamed "Lurch" by his colleagues at the Yard after a character in a popular American television series, then being shown in England. When he spoke, his big hands made awkward gestures and his eyes rolled one way and another to create a variety of weird expressions.

The three men stood at the far end of the pub, near the fireplace, where a large German shepherd sat on the dark-blue rug. Franklin reported that the Yard had identified the three members of the counterfeiting ring Mark had so far met. Dave Blake, the cabdriver, was a distributor who obviously had been out of his depth in trying to put together a deal, so he had gone to the next level, in the person of Ron Schneider, the cockney who also drove a taxicab. Ron lived in Bromley, Kent, with a wife and a twenty-year-old daughter. He was a reasonably successful hustler, but on a lower scale than he'd implied. He had no criminal record and his connections to the British under-world were limited, but the police warned he might be un-stable and prone to violence.

Brad Lewis, whom Mark and Jim had hoped was the Magician, ran a profitable taxicab company with a fleet of thirteen cabs. Again, no criminal background. Perhaps the Magician had chosen him precisely because of his status in the business community, not to mention the fact that his taxi drivers were in the perfect position to act as distribu-tors. (Ron was one of those drivers, but Dave worked for a different cab company.) The drivers were mobile, with a legitimate way to meet with buyers without causing the slightest suspicion.

Franklin mentioned that the Yard was reluctant to put Dave, Ron, and Brad under surveillance, lest they become suspicious and withdraw from dealing with Mark. Most of the squad detectives felt that Brad Lewis would never be able to bring the Magician into a deal in person. Perhaps Brad himself could be arrested for possession, although it was unlikely that *he* made any deliveries personally. Maybe the £25,000 worth of forged notes would be deliv-ered by Ron, in which case the Yard could arrest *him* and try to enlist his help as an informant.

"That sounds ridiculous," Mark said as they ate sand-wiches in the crowded pub. "Why arrest *anybody* when there's still the slightest chance of going further? If you act too soon, the operation is dead."

"Once the delivery is made," Franklin said, "we'll be faced with the problem of how you pay for it."

"The Yard'll supply the money, won't it?"

Franklin's eyes rolled upward. "Not a chance. It's never been done."

"But Christ, isn't the Bank of England worried?"

"Oh, you bet they are. The officials of that august body are very, very sensitive. They're in a right twit about it. The notes are still turning up at a whack of fifty thousand quid a week. Nobody knows when it'll end. There's a bloody panic. Some think it's the IRA."

"Do you?" Mark asked.

"Could be," said Lurch. "But in my experience, forgers are all egotists. They work for themselves. Once in a great while, a genius comes along—a man who's motivated more by pride than greed. That may be the situation in this case. The man's note is a real beauty, all right."

Mark was gratified when the sergeant expressed his personal opinion that Operation Wellington offered the best chance of "getting the forger's hand on the paper."

"This man is unusually cautious," Franklin went on. "He could easily do more volume, but he's unloading at a controlled level. He's got so many others out in front of him that none of our snouts have any idea who he is. We feel that southeast London is the source, but the notes are also coming out as far north as Manchester. They're filtering through the system all over the country. The consequences could be terrible, no doubt about it."

Franklin added that the Yard was eager to bring an undercover agent into the picture to deal directly with the Magician, if possible. "Because," he went on, "right now the detectives feel out of control and they're nervous."

"Well," Mark said, "just remember I've told these gobetweens that my money supplier is from Germany. A German national—so he's got to speak the language."

"No problem," Franklin said, adding that the Yard's

German-speaking agent would seek to move the negotiations to the highest level before any real cash had to change hands.

Disappointed that he would be prevented from pursuing the case all the way to its end, Mark said, "Well, look, tell Miller to get his man into it fast, okay? I'm under a lot of pressure about my job. I need to get back to work soon or I'll be fired." If the Yard was so eager to be rid of his involvement, then Mark himself would take the lead in getting out. The hell with it.

"I say," Edward "Lurch" Franklin said as he jostled through the crowd with his fourth beer, "this place is a glue pot. Once you get in here, you're stuck. Cheers," he added with a broad grin as he raised the mug to his lips.

For Brad Lewis, it had allegedly begun early that summer, when he answered the phone in his office at the taxi firm and heard a soft male voice at the other end. The caller, identifying himself as "Lee," said that he had a "business proposition" in mind. Exerting no pressure whatsoever, Lee suggested that Brad go to the London Hilton and pick up a message "for Mr. James Smith" at the desk.

Out of curiosity, Brad went to the Hilton and was given an envelope containing a dozen £5 notes. Only when Lee called again did he learn for sure that the bills were forgeries. Marveling at their similarity to the real thing, and tempted by the prospect of making easy money on the side, Brad expressed his interest in hearing the proposition.

Lee was cautious at first, as if he wanted Brad to be certain that there was no risk involved. "Right now I'm using only three personal contacts," Lee said, "but things have been so successful that I've decided to develop a few more." He had become interested in Brad, he went on, because of the taxicab fleet, which provided a built-in way for pickups and transactions to be made. But Lee had also conducted a "long and careful investigation" of Brad's personal background and current situation. It was important, for example, that Brad was a family man who ran his own business.

"I think I can trust you," Lee said, "becuse you've got a solid life to protect. You're not so small-minded that you would be carried away."

Brad assured him that this assessment of his character was accurate. He was dependable and could be counted on to keep his word. He would never talk to the police or anyone else. If he could make some extra cash without too much trouble, maybe he could be persuaded. But what was it that he must do?

Lee outlined a set of strict rules and procedures that, he stressed, had to be followed exactly and without exception. Brad was to form his own, private distribution team of no more than five members, each of whom would sell to other distributors. The effect would be that of a geometric progression, creating as many as three dozen middlemen below Brad alone, not to mention hundreds of street-level passers who would actually use the notes in shops and stores.

But in practice, for Brad, it would be a very simple setup. He should select his key people one by one; and they, in turn, would line up deals. Brad would never, never meet with any "buyer" himself. Also, no deals could be for any more than a thousand forged fivers at a time. This would prevent any middleman from making a huge profit all at once and running away with it. Instead, distributors would be motivated to keep arranging new transactions and returning for more and more shipments.

Brad himself would never have to handle the counterfeit money, either. Pickups would be made by his key distributors instead. Therefore, Brad would be totally insulated, or at least one step removed, from anything illegal. And, Brad thought, it meant that Lee himself was even further removed.

Brad chose one of his own taxi drivers, Ron Schneider, as his first distributor. The loud-mouthed cockney had boasted about knowing an assortment of shady contacts, so it was easy enough to get him involved. Within a few days, Ron reported that he himself had lined up an order for five hundred notes.

Having no way to make contact with Lee on his own, Brad was forced to wait for a phone call. When it came, he said, "There's a buyer who wants five hundred models." Lee calmly replied that a "shipment" of that amount would be ready within twenty-four hours at Victoria Station. Meanwhile, Brad should wait for further instructions.

The next day, a delivery man arrived with a package containing a mass of tissue paper and, inside, a locker key with a number on it. Brad gave it to Ron, who went to Victoria Station and retrieved the carefully wrapped shipment of notes from the locker. By evening, Ron returned to say that the deal had been concluded; and he brought the payoff money with him.

Lee expected to receive his guaranteed share of the payoff money—£1 per note or, in this case, £500—before he would approve another transaction. He gave out each shipment on credit, but only when a "firm deal" had been lined up in advance. The commissions earned by Brad and Ron depended on the price paid by the buyer. In this instance, for five hundred forged fivers, Ron had received £2 per note or £1000, half of which would have to go to Lee. Ron and Brad split the remaining half, winding up with £250 apiece.

When Brad had Lee's payoff money, he waited for another phone call and the familiar voice asking, "How's the weather?" Brad replied that the weather was fine; and Lee instructed him to proceed to the front of the British Museum on Great Russell Street. When he did so, he was approached by a distinguished-looking, white-haired gentleman of perhaps forty-five, with sparkling blue eyes and a confident smile. Lee was about five-eleven, no taller, and as they shook hands, Brad noticed that the Magician's face was tanned and rugged-looking, as if he might be a wealthy outdoorsman of some sort. Although, Brad thought, if he really is the forger, he must have spent hours upon hours in his darkroom and printing shop to perfect his handiwork.

"So," Lee said according to a prepared script, "you're feeling well?"

"Yes," Brad replied, handing over the envelope containing Lee's £500 share of the payoff money. With a swift gesture, Lee stuffed the envelope into his jacket pocket, smiled, and turned away, heading for a silver-and-gray Rolls-Royce parked at the curb.

And so it went, through July and August and September. Brad was making a decent profit, but it occurred to him that Lee was raking in a fortune if each of his "personal contacts" was returning a pound for every note printed and sold.

In early October, Ron started causing trouble. The volatile cockney claimed that one of *his* distributors (Dave Blake, whom Brad had never met) knew a "wealthy American" who was demanding to buy twenty thousand notes all at once, for £1.50 per note or £30,000. Even if they had to give Dave a slice of their own commissions, and even at such a low price, it would be an incredibly large deal. It meant that Lee could earn £20,000 while Brad, Ron, and Dave divided £10,000 among themselves.

In one transaction, they would make almost as much as they'd earned up to that point.

Ron said he had met personally with the American, whose name was Mark, and at one point he brought back a gold bar that he said Mark had given him. Brad told him to return it—only English currency would be acceptable—and knowing Lee's strict rules, he instructed the cockney to tell the American that the deal would have to be done in twenty separate transactions; but Ron returned to say that the American was adamant about one big deal. Every day for a week, the cockney kept pleading and yelling about how stupid they were to let such an opportunity slip through their fingers. But Brad stood firm: the American could do a series of one-thousand-note deals or none at all.

After Ron's constant badgering, Brad went against a cardinal rule that Lee had given him by agreeing to confront the American in person. At the meeting in the Carlton Tower Hotel, the American seemed on the level. He also made a lot of sense, to the point where Brad dropped his pose and impulsively gave his word that he could persuade "the printer" to allow four separate transactions of five thousand notes apiece.

Now the American was expecting his first delivery this afternoon. Brad had no way to telephone Lee, so it was necessary to wait for his call. When it came, Brad took the plunge: "Listen, I haven't bothered you with this yet, but there's a wealthy American who wants twenty thousand models at one-pound-fifty apiece in a single deal."

"You know the proper size of a purchase," Lee said.

"The man says he'll settle for five thousand models instead."

"That's still five times too many."

Brad was barely able to hide the disappointment in his voice. "I just thought I'd let you know what's on the table. I figured you might not want to pass it up."

"I appreciate your concern."

"He has an organization that can buy almost any amount."

"Who is this American?"

"Name is Mark. Lives in Knightsbridge. He may have some heavy connections."

For the first time ever, Brad heard Lee laughing at the other end. "Connections," the mysterious man said with another laugh. "Connections to the Old Bill, you mean."

The reference to the police suddenly sent Brad into a panic. Was it possible? "Do you think so?"

"Of course," came the voice. "They've probably brought in the Secret Service or the FBI. Forget the whole thing."

Brad was fairly certain by now that Lee was the actual printer. He also knew from Ron, who did have connections with an assortment of criminal types, that the forger was called the Magician by street-level passers who felt that the quality of the counterfeit notes had been achieved by nothing short of magic. If Lee was, in fact, the Magician, he probably had the ability to sense a trap.

"Tell your people to be very careful," the voice was saying in a relaxed, confident manner. "You haven't met with this American personally, have you?"

Brad hesitated. "I saw him yesterday morning," he admitted after a long pause. "I felt I should, because of the quantity he wanted."

"You broke a rule," Lee said.

"I'm sorry."

"We may have to terminate our arrangement, Brad. Until you've straightened this out, you won't receive any shipments from me. No more deals. You're going to have to resolve things with this American before you can do business with anybody else."

Brad's insides were growing weaker by the moment. He said, "How can I find out if he's the Old Bill?"

"Well, that may be fairly simple. I could arrange for you to have someone pick up a thousand models with thirty different serial numbers. That should be impressive. See if he'll pay for them."

"I don't think he'll go for it."

"Tell him he has to show good faith. If he won't let cash out of his hands, you've sussed him out as the Old Bill."

"How is that?"

"Because the police won't allow him to pay cash. If he doesn't, you'll have called his bluff."

Following Brad's instructions, Ron Schneider picked up the package of one thousand forged £5 notes. The amount was only one-fifth of what Mark was expecting. Ron recalled that Brad had warned him to "play it safe" by dropping off the package without Mark's knowledge. Something about Brad's manner had alerted him to possible danger. "Get it into the house and get out of there," Brad had said. Well, he would try. He could not bear the thought of going to jail.

The question, assuming Mark to be on the level, was whether he would accept such a "small" delivery. There was every reason to believe he would be furious. Brad had promised to deliver five thousand notes or none at all, so now Ron felt like the messenger about to have his head chopped off for bringing the bad news. He drove into Wilton Place at four o'clock, half an hour before the scheduled delivery, and stuffed the parcel under his blue-denim jacket as he walked to the house.

Mark answered the doorbell. "You're early. I'll go get Jim."

"Wait a minute," Ron said, "Let's talk first."

"What for? I'm expecting to receive a delivery in the back of a taxicab. That was our agreement."

"Can I come in and talk to you?"

"All right. But I told you—I don't want to meet in the house anymore. This is the last time."

In the dining room, Ron blurted out, "Brad says the man won't release any more than a thousand notes."

"Here we go again," Mark said. "Then there's no deal."

Ron acted equally annoyed. "Why the fuck not? Why can't you do it?"

"We've been through this shit already!"

Ron sat down. As he spoke, he let the parcel slide from inside his jacket until he held it in his lap under the table. "We've put in a lot of work on this," he said. "Why don't we make *some* money on it?"

"I don't have time for little deals."

"My cut's going right out the window!" Ron pleaded.

"Your man is stalling—not me!"

"I'm caught in the crossfire!"

"Just have Brad call me and explain how he can go back on his word."

"His hands are tied!"

"Well, too bad. I'm accustomed to dealing with people who make their own decisions."

The cockney turned to one side and carefully placed his package on the floor beneath the chair.

After Ron left, Mark walked back into the dining room to watch him drive off. The last thing he felt like doing was going upstairs to tell Jim the bad news. Now the forgery-squad detectives could say they'd been right all along: Operation Wellington was a bad joke. As he turned away from the window, Mark spotted a package on the rug. Lifting it up, he was seized by a fear that it might be an explosive. He gently set it on the long table and carefully undid the wrapping. The parcel contained a bundle of £5 notes in ten separately wrapped, transparent bags.

"Hey, Jim!" he called upstairs. "Come down and see what I've got!"

Each bag contained a hundred notes or £500 in forged currency. The total of £5000, spread out on the dining-room table, was impressive. "The only trouble," Jim said, "is that you can't pay for it."

"Why not?" Mark demanded.

"The Yard's regulations prohibit us from paying out real cash."

"But I'm acting as an undercover man! I'm supposed to be posing as a buyer! How can I do that if I can't pay any money?"

"I don't know," Jim said. "I just don't know."

"Look, Jim, the Magician is trying to call my bluff! He's made a shrewd move! If I don't pay, he won't let Brad proceed any further. We'll be at a dead end!"

When the phone rang, Mark picked it up and was startled to hear Brad's voice on the other end of the line. "What's the big idea, Brad?"

"What do you mean?"

"I found your little package, man. Ron dropped it at my house! We were supposed to do the exchange in a taxicab, remember?"

"Why don't you just pay for it and show your good faith?"

Mark had an impulse to go along by producing cash out of his own pocket, but then he remembered that this was the Yard's game, not his. And under its rules, to "show good faith" was impossible. He yelled back, "You just get the hell over here and pick up this shit!"

"But why?"

"I was expecting twenty-five thousand pounds," Mark roared. "And furthermore, I don't want any stuff in this house!"

"Mark, I'm doing everything I can—"

"Look, Brad, you're exposing me to terrible danger!"

"We just wanted you to see all the serial numbers. There are thirty of them. I thought you'd be impressed."

"I'll be impressed when you show me the right quantity. So right now you get this shit out of my house! I'm a sitting duck over here!"

"Why are you so nervous, Mark?"

"I'm not nervous, I'm angry! You said it would happen in a cab! I'm sitting here with five thousand pounds in forged currency in my house while you're nice and safe!"

"Well," Brad said, "if you're upset with five thousand pounds, what would you be like if I'd had twenty-five thousand dropped off?"

"I'd be five times as upset," Mark shouted into the phone.

"So you're not going to pay for the stuff?"

"Hell, no! Come and pick it up!"

There was a silence, then Brad replied, "Okay, Mark. I'll send a cabdriver with instructions. Just give him the parcel."

Now it was Jim's turn to pick up the phone. He called the Yard and reported to Superintendent Miller that he and Mark were in possession of £5000 in forged D.5/2 notes.

"We can't let you pay for it," Miller replied.

"I know," Jim said. "But Yarry made a brilliant move."

"He did? What move is that?"

"He told them to come and take back the notes. That way, we can keep the case going. A cabdriver is coming to pick up the package."

"We'll have to arrest him."

Jim held the phone in silence. "But then Mark and I will be totally exposed!"

"Well," Miller replied, "we can't in good conscience allow any forged currency to get away from us. It's against every rule we've got."

Jim was sick with disgust. Mark had skirted one of the Yard's rules only to wind up trapped by another. First he had been forbidden to pay for the notes; now he was being prevented from giving them back. "So what do we do?" Jim asked.

"Just stay in the house with Yarry. We'll carry on from here. If the driver picks up the notes, we'll be waiting for him."

It was seven-fifteen in the evening. From the second-floor window of the drawing room, Mark and Jim gazed down at Wilton Place. They could see the police already moving into position in unmarked cars. One vehicle was hidden in the driveway of Saint Paul's Church across the street, behind a brick wall. Another car was on the dead end side street next to the Berkeley Hotel, facing Wilton Place. Two cars were ready to block an escape attempt via Knightsbridge and Hyde Park. At the opposite end of the block was a "static van" filled with plainclothes officers.

Mark shook his head. "Seems there's a cop under every manhole."

Jim nodded as they gazed down at the scene. "And behind every bush."

"Well, my friend, we're about to see the Yard in action. An army of thousands is about to pounce on a lowly cab-driver, while the Magician goes completely free!"

"Shit," Jim muttered.

"All for a five-thousand-pound package of bogus bills," Mark went on. "When the Magician hears about the Great Taxi Bust, he'll split a gut laughing."

Jim cursed again under his breath. "Let's just hope they don't move in right away," he said. "They should at least

97

follow the driver to see where he drops off the stuff. Maybe they'll get Brad at the other end."

At seven-thirty, a black London taxicab flashing its On Call sign came into the block and stopped just past the doorway, between No. 20 and No. 22 Wilton Place. When the driver emerged, Mark and Jim could see that it was a young man in his early twenties.

"It's him," Mark whispered.

The young taxi driver stood on the sidewalk, staring at the door to the adjacent house.

"He's got the wrong address," Jim said.

"Jesus, maybe he'll go away!"

"Let's hope so."

Time seemed to freeze. Then without warning the entire block erupted with movement. To Mark, it was akin to watching a play or movie in which all the mannequins abruptly come alive, leaping out of the painted scenery. Several cars converged on the taxicab from all directions. Plainclothes cops poured out from the van, from the cars, from everywhere, surrounding the startled driver. Police radios and walkie-talkies were screeching and some thirty officers seemed to be shouting all at the same time.

"Oh, no!" Mark cried. "What are they *doing?* He hasn't even picked up the notes yet!"

The young driver was tackled and knocked off his feet, then thrown against his taxicab. Two detectives searched him while the others were running about in confusion.

Amid the commotion below, Sergeant Ed Franklin was in a state of shock. The police hadn't even waited for the driver to pick up the notes, much less tried to follow him to his destination. Some officer on the radio had gotten jumpy and had yelled out an order to "attack"—and all hell had broken loose.

Lurch Franklin, now earning his nickname more

than ever, glanced over at the door of 22 Wilton Place, adjacent to Mark's house. The door opened and a middle-aged couple emerged, arm-in-arm. The man was dressed in a tuxedo and the woman wore an evening gown with a fur coat. The couple gazed at the chaotic scene in bewilderment.

Franklin walked over to them and said, "Don't worry—I'm with Scotland Yard. Everything's under control. Can I help you?"

"Officer," the man said with typical British reserve, "my wife and I are on our way to the theater, for an opening-night performance. Could you ring us *another* taxi?"

Franklin stared at the couple. "Did you order a cab to pick you up?"

"Yes, we did. But now I'm afraid we'll be late for the curtain."

Franklin marched over to the cabdriver, who was protesting through his tears that he had no idea of what was happening to him or why, and yelled above the confusion, "Were you on call?"

"Yes, sir," the young man said, his voice shaking uncontrollably.

"To what address?"

"Twenty-two Wilton Place."

"Twenty-*two*?"

"Yes, sir."

When Mark heard they had jumped on the wrong cabdriver, he turned to Jim and said, "Look, if the counterfeiters are watching this place, it's over. That was enough commotion to wake the dead. But maybe they're not anywhere near here and there's still time—"

The phone rang. "Mark? It's Brad. I'm about to send the driver. Just let him pick up the package."

With a surge of excitement, and not knowing what else to say, Mark shouted into the phone, "Brad, don't send anybody *near* the place! The street is full of cops—I don't know what the hell's happening! I'm getting the notes out of here! Jim's taking the stuff out the back and over the roof! Call me back in an hour! If there's no answer, you can assume I've been arrested!"

When he had hung up, Brad Lewis was mystified. It seemed that Mark had been genuinely upset, even frantic. Was it just a ploy, so the Yard could hold on to the package of forged notes? Or was Mark on the level, actually afraid of being caught? An hour later, he called back and listened for the slightest false note in Mark's voice:

"Listen, Brad, it's okay. I sent Jim out with the stuff, so it's safe. We really didn't have to worry—it was a bomb scare at the Argentine embassy just down the block."

Brad listened, trying to weigh what he was hearing. A bomb scare?

"That was a close one," Mark was saying. "With all the embassies in this neighborhood, you never know what the hell's going on. In the past few weeks, there've been three explosions—right nearby! One even shook the house. Anyway, all the cops out there had me scared shitless. It looked like World War Three."

"Well," Brad said, reserving his judgment, "it had nothing to do with us. We've never been tailed—we'd know it if we had been. It's cool at this end. By the way, I didn't send the cab over."

"Good," Mark said. "Listen, I'm willing to pay you for the package after all, if it means we can get on with the larger deal."

Brad relaxed a bit as he held the phone. If Mark was willing to pay cash, he might be for real. It could be that he really did want to get everything done in one lump; he might have been genuinely upset over having to go through the risk of too many transactions; and perhaps he actually *had* been nervous sitting there with a package of forged notes in his house. After all, Brad thought, he warned me when he thought there was trouble. It was possible that the Magician had been cautious to a fault. Proof of Mark's trustworthiness would come when he delivered £1500 in cash.

"How do you want to make the payment?" Brad asked.

"Let's meet tomorrow morning at the Carlton Tower. Nine o'clock in the lobby."

"All right," Brad said. "But now it's up to you to pay before we go on."

Tuesday, 15 October

In a strange, unexpected way, Mark found himself in sympathy with Brad. According to the rules imposed upon him by the Magician, he had done his best. He had delivered a thousand forged notes, as many as he had been allowed to unload, and now he expected to be paid. Undoubtedly the forger was pressuring Brad to show some tangible results before letting him proceed with negotiations for any larger deal. The key, Mark thought, is to help Brad, not hinder him.

Because there was no money to help him with, it was imperative to maintain an attitude of self-righteousness, to keep Brad off-balance. As the Carlton Tower meeting began this morning, with Ron Schneider and Jim Goldie looking on, Mark skirted the topic of payment by leading off with an attack: "What the hell went wrong, Brad? You owe me an explanation. I was expecting to receive five thousand notes in the back of a cab, remember?"

"The printer wouldn't do it," Brad replied. "I talked to

the man until I was hoarse, but he just doesn't trust the big deals. I'm sorry, Mark, but that's what we're stuck with."

The four men were seated once again at a table in the rear of the coffee lounge, trying to keep their voices as low as possible. Ron Schneider leaned toward Mark with a scowl on his face and rasped, "Look, we've been fucking about on this deal for two weeks and we've still got fuck-all to show for it!"

Now it was Jim's turn. If Mark and Brad were equals on one level, then the Scotsman and the cockney could negotiate with each other on another. "Wait a minute," Jim snapped at Ron. "If anyone fucked up, it was you. What was the idea of dropping the five grand at Mark's house like that? Didn't you realize what you were doing?"

Ron bristled. "We wanted you to see the numbers on the notes. If you saw how many there are, you *have* to believe there's the quantity you want."

"That's right," Brad said to Mark.

"We don't like doing business that way," Jim retorted, but still aiming his remarks at Ron. "The exchange was to take place in a taxi. That was *your* suggestion and—"

Brad interrupted and said, "Mark, I'm sorry. When I spoke to the printer and he wouldn't part with the twenty-five thousand pounds, I thought the next best thing would be to let you see the five grand. What else could I do?"

"So now you want fifteen hundred pounds from me?"

"Mark, it's absolutely necessary. There's no other way we can get it off center. The printer himself wanted you to see the serial numbers. Thirty of 'em, Mark."

"So?"

Brad explained that for each different serial number, the Magician had been required to make a separate printing plate with just the number on it. It was logical to assume, therefore, that each new number represented a substantial "runoff" of notes using that plate. Beyond that, the existence of varied numbers on the forged bills was a big selling point. Distributors could boast to potential buyers that the printer had gone to great lengths to insure a proper "mix" for street-level passers, who were reluctant to use several bills at a time if the numbers on them were all the same.

"Now," Brad went on, "we're faced with a choice—either you give back the load or pay the fifteen hundred."

"The money is no object, Brad. It's not a question of that."

"Okay, then. As soon as you pay me, I can establish your credibility with the printer and we can get on to bigger things."

"I'd love to pay you right now," Mark said truthfully. "What I need," he went on, "is assurance that your man has the balance. In other words, is he sitting somewhere with ninety-five thousand pounds of what I want? Otherwise, this puny deal isn't worth my time *or* my money."

Brad shook his head in frustration. "Of course the man has that amount," he said. "What the hell do you need, a signed contract?"

Ron looked as if he were about to lift up the coffee table out of sheer anger. Instead he came out with a loud, hoarse whisper, speaking so intensely that the muscles on his face were twitching. "Don't worry, Mark. Believe me, there's whatever amount you want. This man is a genius!"

"You've already told me that."

"But he *is*, Mark. I've never had any contact with him," Ron went on, "but Brad can tell you—the Bank of England would give a million pounds to put him out of business! He's a perfectionist! You take my word for it—they'll *never* catch him. He's like the elusive Pimpernel!"

Mark had to stop himself from laughing out loud. The "elusive Pimpernel" referred to the foppish hero of *The Scarlet Pimpernel,* the 1905 romantic novel about the French Revolution written by Baroness Emmuska Orczy, the English novelist. There had been at least three British film versions of the tale, featuring actors such as Leslie Howard and David Niven. The leading character used the assumed name of the "Scarlet Pimpernel" and rescued others from mortal danger by smuggling them across the border. And, of course, there was the familiar verse:

> We seek him here, we seek him there,
> Those Frenchies seek him everywhere.
> Is he in heaven?—Is he in hell?
> That damned elusive Pimpernel?

Had Ron Schneider seen one of those old movies? Even more intriguing, Mark thought, was that the "pimpernel" was a plant or herb whose flowers closed up at the approach of stormy weather—an apt description of the mysterious Magician of *this* romantic adventure now in progress.

"The elusive Pimpernel," Jim echoed, winking at Mark as he excused himself to go to the men's room.

"That's him," Ron said in earnest. "And he's smarter than all of Scotland Yard."

"Really?" Mark replied.

"He's way ahead of everybody," Brad joined in. "He knows what the Bank of England is planning before it happens."

"How do you mean?"

"Well, he called me late last night. He said the Bank is going to put out a new ten-pound note very soon. That's classified information! And he's already got the design!"

"You're kidding," Mark said.

"No," Brad went on. "He says the Government's new ten-pound bill is set to hit the street next month. He'll have his own identical note on the market by then or early December. He wants to time it for the Christmas shopping rush."

Mark was stunned. What he was hearing would be extremely interesting to the Yard and the Bank of England, to say the least.

"He's a wealthy man," Brad continued, "so he doesn't jump until he wants to. He's very thorough and professional, which is why he's never been caught. Knows the whole history of counterfeiting and how many people have been nicked and why."

Ron broke in: "He's the only man who's had two lots and never a sniff."

"What do you mean?" Mark asked him.

"There was a one-pound forgery two years ago. He did that and let it die without a sniff. Now he's come back with the five-pound note. And the tenner is on its way."

As Jim returned to the table, Mark realized that they could possibly use this blockbusting piece of information as a wedge to pressure the Yard. Meanwhile, a new meeting was arranged for eight o'clock that evening at Mr. Chow restaurant in Knightsbridge. Brad made a persuasive, pleading speech about how he would expect to receive his payment at that time, adding that it would be the only way to convince the Magician to release more of the counterfeit notes. "It's a paltry sum," he continued, "but everything else depends on it."

Jim called the Yard and got Superintendent Miller on the line. In an even tone of voice, he made it clear that the £1500 was an absolute necessity if Operation Wellington were to continue. The counterfeiters were demanding to have it that evening.

"Impossible," Miller said. "There is no way on God's earth that we can part with any money to make a buy. I've told you over and over."

Listening on the other extension, Mark found it laughable that while Brad was trying to keep the Magician involved in the deal, he and Jim were in much the same position with the Yard. The Magician was being offered the biggest transaction of his career, yet for his own reasons he was holding back—at least until he saw some cash as evidence of good faith; and the Yard was being offered its best opportunity to solve the D.5/2 investigation, yet was also refusing to give in.

Losing all patience, Mark broke into the phone conversation: "Superintendent Miller?"

"I say—is that you, Mr. Yarry?"

"You're damn right it is. Listen, you're being ridiculous."

"There are no precedents for paying out money."

"But how can you expect us to go on with any kind of credibility if you're not helping us? You're not giving me any tools to do the job! What's a lousy fifteen hundred pounds if it means success or failure?"

"You're not saying you'll guarantee success if you pay the money, are you?"

"No, but I'll guarantee *failure*, if I *don't* pay it."

"Mr. Yarry, the Yard has every expectation of solving this case and—"

Mark slammed the receiver down.

On his own extension, Jim frantically suggested to Superintendent Miller that he meet with Mark on some common ground to discuss other ways of keeping the case alive. After considerable effort, he got Miller to agree to be at Waterloo Station, the main railroad terminal for trains to the south of England, at two o'clock that afternoon.

Mark arrived by cab and met alone with Miller in the bar on the station's second floor. Huddling in a corner, they argued for nearly an hour but got nowhere. Mark deliberately brought up the news, which he had kept to himself so far, that the forger apparently had a contact inside the Bank of England. Miller looked startled, but then he smirked as if such a thing were impossible. "Well," Mark added, "maybe it would interest you to know that your own government has a new ten-pound note in the works. The *forger* knows, so you might as well, too. He's got secret information that the new note will be issued in December. The forger has his *own* in the works and he's planning to release a flood of counterfeits during the Christmas-shopping rush!"

"The question," Miller said, "is whether under *any* circumstances we can give you some 'buy' money. And the answer, Mr. Yarry, is no."

In exasperation, Mark suggested that in lieu of real cash it might be helpful if Miller could get him a small piece of the offical note paper used by the Bank of England.

"Maybe two inches by three inches," Mark said. "Nothing that the forger can use to make a note with, but something to show him. If he thinks I can get hold of the actual paper, through my organization, he'd be ecstatic. I could offer to make payment for the entire deal with bank-note paper. He might be tempted, you know?"

"Maybe," Miller said, "but it's out of the question."

"Not even a tiny swatch of paper?"

"Absolutely not."

"Well," Mark said in a fury, "I just don't understand it.

What do I tell Brad tonight when he asks for his money?"

"You'll think of something," Miller said.

"Well, *you* tell the Bank of England that I'm looking forward to seeing the new ten-pound note in December!"

Miller frowned. "Are you serious?" he asked.

"That's for you to find out," Mark replied. "Have an especially Merry Christmas, sir," he added sarcastically as he walked away.

When he returned to Wilton Place, Mark immediately told Jim about the £10 note for the first time. "I knew you'd be required to report it to them," he said, "so I was saving it for the right moment. By the expression on Miller's face, it may have had the desired effect. I'm sorry, Jim, but I didn't want you to be compromised."

Jim shrugged. "Well," he said with a faint grin, "they're right—I can't control you."

The two men laughed as they walked into the kitchen for a beer.

As an additional move, Mark placed a call to Sir Leslie O'Brien, the former Governor of the Bank of England, whom he had met a few years before at a conference sponsored by the *Institutional Investor*. Perhaps if O'Brien knew the facts and what was at stake, he would intercede and try to use his influence at the highest level of Government.

Jim stood nearby with a worried look on his face; but Sir Leslie, who was currently working for an investment-banking firm, could not be reached. He was in the United States on business. "Could you have him ring me as soon as possible?" Mark asked the secretary at the other end. "Tell him it's urgent that I speak with him. It's a matter of national importance. A security matter involving the Bank of England and Scotland Yard."

By now it was nearly five o'clock. Carried along by his own mementum, and with all options disappearing, Mark paced around in his study while Jim sat helplessly waiting for the next surprise. "Who is at the highest level?" Mark asked.

Jim looked bewildered. "The Commissioner, but—"

"No, I mean even higher."

"Well, the Metropolitan Police are under the jurisdiction of the Home Secretary."

"I'm going to call him."

"Christ, Mark, you can't do that!"

But he was already in motion, dialing information for Home Secretary Roy Jenkins. "If by some miracle I can talk to him," Mark said, "I'm sure I'll convince him to get us that money."

"Well," Jim said with a weak laugh, "here goes my career."

"*You're* not making the call, *I* am. It's not your fault. I mean, you can just say there was no way to stop me. Which," Mark added with a smile, "there isn't."

Roy Jenkins' private secretary came on the line. Mark gave his name and launched into his plea. "I'm an American involved in assisting Scotland Yard in a counterfeiting case. I'm having enormous problems here. I'm not at all satisfied with the action the Yard is taking. I'd like to speak to the Home Secretary, please." After some hesitation at the other end, Mark added, "Listen, if you don't believe me, I have a police officer standing next to me right now. He's working on the case. I'll put him on the phone and he'll verify to you that this is not a crank call."

He held the telephone out to Jim Goldie, who by now had turned pale. Until this ordeal had begun, Jim had followed the police regulations and procedures to the letter. Now he was about to go right over the heads of Superintendent Miller and Commander Grant and even the Commissioner, to the Home Secretary's office, and he could already imagine the repercussions.

"Hello," he said with a quiver in his voice, "my name is Detective Constable James Goldie. I'm assigned to the National Center for Suppression of Counterfeit Currency. What Mr. Yarry told you is true—he's working on a case for Scotland Yard."

The secretary, a man, replied that he would call the Yard for confirmation and that Jenkins himself would be informed. Jim hung up and waited for the explosion that was bound to come. "I'll give it five minutes," he said, checking his watch. Within four minutes, the phone rang.

Mark answered, then heard Superintendent Miller's voice: "Let me speak to Mr. Goldie, please." Miller's mood, Mark thought, was anything but mellow. He handed the phone to Jim.

"This is Goldie," Jim said, already wincing.

"Jesus Christ!" Miller shouted. "Can't you control that Yarry? Do you know what he's done? He's called the Home Secretary!"

"Yes, sir."

"He's making us look like fools over here!" Miller screamed. "He told Jenkins' office that he thinks we can't do our jobs! Why can't you control the bloody Yank?"

"Sir, I can't stop him from using his own phone."

"What if he decides to ring up the newspapers? The guy is a fucking time bomb!"

"Sir, he wouldn't call the papers. He just—"

From across the room, Mark yelled at the top of his voice, "Oh, yes I would! I just might! The *Daily Telegraph* would love to print how the Yard is blowing everything for fifteen hundred lousy pounds!"

"What's he saying?" Miller asked.

"Nothing, sir," Jim said into the phone.

Miller went on to report that the Home Secretary's office had been extremely upset over the Yarry phone call. The Yard had been forced to answer a number of questions: What's going on over there? Why is an American working for Scotland Yard? What if he gets shot? And so forth, until Miller had felt compelled to reply that Yarry was being taken off the case.

"We're bringing in our own agent tonight," he said. "Yarry will take him to Mr. Chow and introduce him to the go-betweens as his money supplier. From there on, our man will take over. I want Yarry out of it! Completely!"

"One moment, sir," Jim said. He cupped his hand over the mouthpiece and whispered to Mark, "They're sending in an undercover agent."

"Let me talk to him," Mark said. He grabbed the phone. "This is Yarry."

"Mr. Yarry, we—"

"Listen, I want to see this guy. He has to speak German When do I meet him?"

"What time is your dinner?" Miller asked.

"Eight o'clock."

"He'll be at your house by seven. I'll bring him over myself."

"Just don't wear your raincoat."

"What?"

"Never mind," Mark said. "Look, I need time to brief this guy, so we can coordinate our stories."

"Don't worry, you'll meet him."

"The idea," Mark went on rapidly, "is that I'm working for a big organization in the States, but my main contact in Europe is this German national who's a successful businessman. I've talked to him about the deal and he's interested. He's come across from Germany to buy a large amount of forged currency. Got that?"

"I understand," Miller said in an annoyed tone of voice. "We *do* know what we're doing, Mr. Yarry."

"He has to *look* German and *speak* German," Mark said. "And for God's sake, he shouldn't look like a cop."

"Well, this particular man—"

"What's his name?"

"Edgar. He's coming from the Special Branch. A very experienced man. He's been in this type of situation a thousand times."

"All right," Mark said, suddenly growing weary and even feeling glad that his role would soon be over. "But Jim is still on the case, right?"

"Oh, yes. He'll be working for the German. You'll be out of it."

"Fine," Mark mumbled. "Send your man."

By seven o'clock all of London was enveloped by fog and drizzle. Superintendent Miller arrived—wearing, of course, his wrinkled gray raincoat—and came upstairs to the study with Edgar, the undercover agent. Edgar was about fifty years old, a squat, balding, overweight man who hardly seemed like a German national. Neither Mark nor Jim said a word. They stared at Edgar incredulously, each wondering what the catch might be.

"Do you speak German?" Mark asked.

"He doesn't need to," Miller snapped. "He knows how to handle himself."

"Have you ever *been* to Germany?"

Edgar nervously shook his head. "I 'ave been to France," he said—in a cockney accent!

"Excuse me, Edgar," said Mark. He took Superintendent Miller by the arm and marched him into the drawing room, kicking the door shut behind them. "What's the big idea?" he said in a low voice, trying to contain his rage.

112

"I don't follow you."

"He's supposed to be a German national!"

"Just because you say so?"

"Superintendent Miller, if you take that man and send him in there, I'm going to the newspapers and telling 'em the sweetest story you ever heard!"

Miller's face grew red. "What are you talking about?"

"Send the man home!" Mark shouted.

"He's a friend of mine," Miller pleaded. "He used to work with me on the vice squad. He's in the Special Branch."

"He's supposed to speak fluent German and be well-traveled in Germany!"

"He can do the job!" Miller shouted back.

The two men returned to the study, where Jim was trying to adapt to the situation by giving Edgar a briefing. Jim mentioned that the Yard's C-11 division had taken numerous pictures of Brad Lewis and Ron Schneider (mostly from inside their "static van" on Wilton Place and outside the Carlton Tower Hotel); but Edgar revealed that he had seen none of the photographs.

"Why not?" Mark said in anger, but neither Edgar nor Superintendent Miller had an asnwer.

Patiently, Jim described Brad's appearance, then Ron's. Edgar's eyes widened and he said, "Hey, I might have questioned one of those guys before! Something to do with stolen goods . . ."

Now the room exploded again, with Mark slamming the wall and yelling at Miller, who shouted back in defense. Mark had visions of the scene in the restaurant if Ron or Brad were to recognize Edgar. All hell would break loose, with the two bogus-money dealers leaping over the tables to escape. Or, if they were armed, Mark himself would be the first target.

It was hurriedly decided that Edgar would proceed to the restaurant right away. He offered to show up with a "friend" and take a table at the far end, near the rest rooms. Meanwhile, Mark would meet with the go-betweens by himself and try to handle the situation until, at some point, he would go to the men's room. He and Edgar would rendezvous at the urinals. Edgar would indicate whether he had recognized either Brad or Ron.

It was raining steadily as Mark hailed a cab and rode the short distance up Sloan Street to Knightsbridge. Approaching Mr. Chow restaurant, he noticed the Yard's unmarked van parked across the street in the darkness. Inside, members of the C-11 division were again taking photos, this time with infrared cameras and telescopic lenses.

Entering the restaurant, Mark figured that this confrontation with the forger's henchmen might well be his last. He took a deep breath, preparing himself for one final effort as a secret agent.

Brad and Ron were waiting for him, neatly dressed in jackets and ties. Mark greeted them and waved to the maître d', who immediately recognized him and said, "Nice to see you, sir."

"Good evening. I'd like a table for three."

"Have you made a reservation?"

"No," Mark said, smiling and maintaining a polite tone.

The maître d' responded with an embarrassed laugh and led them into the dining room. It was crowded, but an extra table was set and the maître d' gestured for Mark and his party to sit down. Brad and Ron kept silent, but it was clear that neither was accustomed to such royal treatment.

"Have a cocktail," Mark told them. "Ordinarily I'd recommend the Peking duck, but you have to order that in advance. If you like, I can order several courses for us. This place has my favorite kind of Chinese food."

While they ordered drinks, Mark glanced up and saw Edgar dining with an attractive, red-haired woman at a table in the rear.

"Do you have our money?" Brad asked.

"Yes," Mark said, "but my people have an objection."

"What's that?"

"Well, first of all, they don't understand why I'm parting with fifteen hundred pounds in real money for five thousand pounds worth of shit."

"What do you mean, 'shit'?"

"Look, it's that question of quantity again. They don't want to get involved unless there's a guarantee that your man has all of what we need."

Brad could hardly control his agitation. "How the hell can I prove it to you?"

"Brad, you don't have to convince *me* anymore. I'm stepping out of this whole thing until I can deal at the top level."

"The printer will never meet with you. Never."

"Well, that's his problem. From now on, you'll have to deal exclusively with Jim. I'm giving him complete authority to make the first payment. If he's satisfied that the quantity exists, he'll pay you."

"Oh, come on, Mark. If *you're* not convinced, how is Jim gonna be satisfied?"

"Well, I have an idea," Mark replied, improvising once again. "How about you guys taking Jim personally to see the rest of the notes?"

"Not possible," Brad said.

"You can take him anywhere you like. Blindfold him, spin him around, and drive him all over London for an hour—I don't care. If Jim comes back and tells me there's ninety-five thousand pounds worth of your notes in existence, then I'll give him the fifteen hundred pounds for the first payment. Otherwise, how do I know that the stuff you gave us isn't just what's left over from another load?"

"He's got a point," Ron said.

"I don't like it," Brad muttered.

But Ron persisted: "All we have to do is give the big Scotsman a peek!"

"Right," Mark said. "As I say, blindfold him and take him anywhere you like."

"It's a bloody good idea," Ron said.

"Well," Brad relented, "when I talk to the printer tomorrow, I'll see if he's willing to make that arrangement."

"He should be," Mark said. "Because there's a lot of money to be made. You guys don't deserve to have it all go down the drain."

"Fucking right," Ron said. "Let's get it moving, Brad."

"I believe in the deal," Mark told them. "And I think you guys have acted in good faith."

Brad nodded. "Yes, we have. We have."

"Which is why I'm ordering Jim to keep on with it, even though I can't afford the time anymore. Let's just hope your man gets some sense into his head, for *your* sake. I'm not asking anything unreasonable, just some assurance that we're talking about more than nickels and dimes."

"It's all up to the printer," Brad said.

"All up to him," Mark echoed. He had kept the deal alive, yet there was still no promise of getting the £1500 from the Yard even if Jim did get a peek at the rest of the forged notes.

When the drinks arrived, Mark excused himself and made his way toward the rear section of the restaurant. Edgar and the red-haired woman were holding hands at their table and whispering with their faces only inches apart. As Mark passed by, he coughed so that Edgar would look up.

Inside the men's room, Mark stood at one of the urinals and waited. He heard Edgar come in behind him. The Special Branch agent walked up to the adjacent urinal and whispered, "Don't know 'em. You can introduce me." Mark reached for a slip of paper in his jacket, thinking that there was no way this man with a cockney accent would have any credibility as a German money supplier. He handed Edgar the previously written message: "Stay Away."

He left the Yard's undercover agent standing at the urinal and returned to his table, where Brad and Ron were waiting. Now there might be time to convince both of them, especially Brad, that he was their friend; and also establish beyond question that he had authority as a now erful member of a worldwide "organization" or crime syndicate. If he could solidify that thought in their minds, Jim's task of carrying on by himself would be that much easier.

With a flourish, Mark ordered several Pekingese dishes for the three of them, plus some excellent white Burgundy. He made it clear, as he talked about the various culinary delights they were about to experience, that he would be picking up the tab; and as they relaxed and began to enjoy themselves, Mark consciously turned his "mirror" toward them, slowly transforming himself into the image that he intuitively knew they wanted to see. It stood to reason that what they desired most was the simplest, safest means of making money. The Magician had secured Brad's loyalty by offering him that same promise; Mark would have to top it. He was competing directly with the Magician for

117

Brad's allegiance. The image that he presented would have to be irresistible.

In the manner of a skillful actor building his character from within, detail by detail, Mark began to construct his fictional organization. He referred to it as "the family"— implying, but never stating, that it was an organized-crime ring associated with the so-called Mafia. He spoke of financiers in Germany, of hit men in Korea, of diamond smugglers in Africa. He mentioned gambling casinos and fabulous hotels and "certain entertainers in our debt," sprinkling his talk with images of Lear jets and beautiful women; and, through it all, he alluded to "big money" that was both guaranteed and hidden from the law. As their eyes followed his every gesture, Mark presented himself as a living example of how someone could prosper from membership in "the family." He dressed well, lived high, traveled at will—all because "the family" had so much power and influence.

Whenever Brad or Ron asked a question, Mark provided what he hoped was a believable answer. The marvelous benefit of having an imaginary organization, he realized, was that it could be molded and shaped into any form at a moment's notice. Nothing was impossible; no aspect of "the family" was too difficult to explain. And, of course, there was a place for everybody:

"You know, Brad, when this deal is over, I might be able to find a spot for you in the family. You too, Ron. We've got a magnificent setup in California. That might be where you guys would fit in."

"Doing what?" Brad asked.

"Well, that's the beauty of it—you don't do a damn thing! See, we've got 'fronts' all over the place. Legitimate businesses. Everything from hotels to restaurants to computer companies. Places where outside money can be invested and channeled. We're always looking for good people to come in and run these operations or just watch over them. Very little work is involved, because they run by themselves. The important thing, for us, is to have loyal people on hand. And from what I've seen, I know you guys can be trusted."

"When I give my word," Ron said, "it's as solid as a rock."

"Well, that's what we need. What *you two* need is better management at the top. You guys shouldn't have to play Mickey Mouse to anybody."

Brad's eyes narrowed. "Is that what you think we're doing?"

"If you want my opinion, yes. Your boss is very, very small-minded."

"He's just being cautious, Mark."

"Yeah, but meanwhile you guys could've made a hell of a lot more money by now. Your man has prevented that. He sits up there in his ivory tower while you go through all this bullshit."

"Well," Brad said with a sigh, "the fact is that the printer doesn't really need me. He has other people who also line up deals." He then explained that three or four contacts like himself were involved, and that *their* distributors, in turn, were making transactions for up to a thousand notes apiece all the time. "So his system is working," Brad went on. "And if I don't make an acceptable deal with you, he might just cut me out altogether."

"So let's get going!" Mark insisted. "You tell your man that he's putting you guys through much too much aggravation and danger. I'll tell you something else," he added, lowering his voice and adopting a secretive, menacing tone. "If my people ever begin to think that this Magician is jerking *me* around . . ."

Brad and Ron stared back at him in silence as if waiting for him to complete his sentence. After a long pause, Ron spoke up in his thickest cockney accent: "Mark, I ain't afraid of dying. It's *living* that scares the shit out of me." "How so?"

"Just getting through the day. Right now I'm trying to save for my daughter's wedding. I want her to have a *decent* wedding, you know? But it'll cost."

For a moment, Mark imagined Ron Schneider's daughter dancing at a wedding reception financed by the proceeds from counterfeit-money deals. He said, "Look, the future for both you guys could be very bright. When our deal goes through, I can get you into the firm without any fuss at all. In fact," he added, now addressing Ron, "if you were in the organization at this moment, my people would foot the *entire bill* for that wedding."

"Jesus," Ron whispered. "You know, when this is over, we should all have dinner with our wives and celebrate."

Brad looked over at his colleague as if he regarded that suggestion as a bit premature. "Let's stick to business," he mumbled.

Mark turned to him. "Of course, Brad, you'd come in at a higher level, because your the key man on this transaction. You're the guy who can make it a success—by convincing the printer."

"Yes, but he's unpredictable."

"Well, if we don't do the deal, I'll have invested a few dollars and some of my time, but you'll have lost a lot more, in terms of the future."

"Yeah, Brad, that's right," said Ron. "This is more than just a deal for its own sake."

Brad nodded but otherwise showed little outward emotion. Unlike Ron, he was not given to revealing much about himself; and through his blue-gray, skeptical eyes, perhaps he also did not see the reflection of his own desires so clearly.

By now, Mark was no longer merely presenting an image. He was "living" his role and working so hard at it that for long stretches of time he forgot all about reality. He was, in fact, part of an international criminal gang; and he was truly attempting to put together a profitable counterfeit-money deal. Brad and Ron were his contacts and friends.

When he paid the check, Mark added an extra-large tip and made sure they saw it. Only when he stood up with them to leave did he fully remember his police role. At that moment he caught a glimpse of Edgar, still seated in the rear of Mr. Chow restaurant, nuzzling up to his female dinner companion.

In the darkness and pouring rain outside the restaurant, Mark watched the two men cross the street and pass right by the police van. They jumped into a parked taxicab and drove off. Brad had promised to be in touch after learning whether the Magician would allow Jim to get a look at the £95,000 worth of additional notes.

Mark waited to hail a cab for himself, but after five minutes of trying he turned and started walking. Within a block he was soaking wet. He had just given a four-hour performance that had left him exhilarated but exhausted. His adventure was over unless compromises came from both the Yard and the forger.

As he walked on in the rain, Mark found himself thinking more about his life in general and how, sometimes, it seemed that nothing in it was real. His wife, his children—they were real, but almost everything else had a quality of impermanence. Everyone plays a role. None of us is what we seem. We all assume "identities" as if they were costumes: a counterfeit-money dealer, a taxi driver, a company executive, a detective, a forger. All these labels signified roles but in no way expressed the truth of anyone in particular. We are all hiding, Mark thought—the way the Magician is, the way I am—behind images that we project to others. And if everyone is pretending and playing a game, then fantasy and reality are always intertwined. To some degree, we all act out a Walter Mitty fantasy—and that's what keeps us sane.

The detectives of Scotland Yard were actually flawed individuals of varying strengths and weaknesses. They were "detectives" almost by accident. The same could be said of the counterfeit-money dealers who were, after all, vulnerable men with innocent families and basic concerns. They worried about making a living and paying for a daughter's wedding. Both Jim Goldie *and* Brad Lewis were individuals with whom Mark had joined in collaboration; and for each relationship, he was playing a new, fictional role. Whatever success he had had so far—as an undercover agent, as a counterfeit-money buyer—merely demonstrated the absurdity of those labels and exposed the "actor" in everyone. As he approached 20 Wilton Place, he was glad to be returning to some degree of offstage privacy. While the Magician continued to soar higher in his flight as a forger, the American retreated from his own performance and temporarily went to ground.

ACT II

Wednesday,
16 October

Detective Sergeant Ed Franklin's hands were gesturing wildly as he recounted the "aggravation and confusion" at the Yard over the previous three days. The laughter that made his wide, darting eyes overflow with tears was infectious. From Lurch Franklin's point of view, there was enough material from this case for an "absolutely side-splitting comedy of errors."

In the midst of the crowd inside the Turks Head pub, Franklin was supposed to be getting a briefing from Mark and Jim, but at the moment he was offering his own version of the recent events in the manner of a stand-up comic. He began with the Yard's realization that the go-betweens had surreptitiously left a thousand forged £5 notes in Mark's dining room. This development had caused Superintendent Miller to remark, "Well, now, this case is becoming a wee bit tasty." Since then, the squad detectives had been calling him Tasty Miller and just plain Tasty. Other nicknames for those working on the D.5/2 investigation had also developed. One lethargic detective was now referred to as Nerve Gas; an inspector, who ran about in confusion most of the time, was dubbed Little Legs; the Crow was named for his long nose that reminded everyone of a beak; and then there was Sludge Gulper, who could pick up a sandwich, swallow it whole, and wash it down with an entire glass of beer in one gulp—a feat which even Franklin could not match.

Tasty Miller had "led the charge" in trying to prevent

the go-betweens from retrieving their forged notes, resulting in the Great Taxi Bust. By some miracle, Operation Wellington had survived. Next had come word from Mark that the forger possessed top-secret knowledge of the Bank of England's plan to issue a new £10 note; and that the forger was going to put a "tenner" of his own on the market.

"We didn't know *anything* about a new tenner," Franklin said with a laugh. "All the guys figured it was a figment of your vivid imagination," he said, poking Mark in the chest. "So Tasty makes a call upstairs, and pretty soon comes word from the Bank that there *is* a new ten-pound note in the works. And now they're all going crazy because the secret got out!"

"Well," Mark said, "do you think the Magician could have a contact inside the Government?"

Franklin nodded. "He must have a man in the Bank. The printers and engravers are sworn to secrecy but there's always a bloke who'll cop a drop," he added, referring to a person who would take a bribe. "So anyway, the Bank is delaying issuance of the new tenner until your 'damned elusive Pimpernel' is nicked."

"Jesus," Mark whispered. "We're talking about the British Government being afraid to put its own money into circulation, all on account of one man."

"He's spinning 'em by the tail and they're having a nervous breakdown," Franklin said. "The ten-pound note was one of the Bank's best-kept secrets. As I say, not even the Yard knew about it."

There was additional pandemonium, Franklin reported, when Home Secretary Roy Jenkins' office called to ask whether it was true that the Yard had enlisted a "bloody Yank" as an undercover agent. "When Tasty realized that Mark had rung Jenkins' office, he nearly had a heart attack on the spot. That was when he decided to bring in Edgar."

126

Why, Mark wanted to know, would the Yard come up with such a poor imitation of a German national?

"Well, I think Miller acted in a bit of haste," Franklin replied with a grin. "He felt the case was so 'tasty' that it'd be nice if he could bring in a friend to share the glory."

"But still," Mark said, "how did he think Edgar could pull it off?"

Franklin drained his beer mug and said, "It's part of an old problem in police circles. The man in the office tends to forget what it's like out in the field. Tasty's a good administrative officer, but he wouldn't be much help as a spy. From what I hear, Edgar was relieved that you didn't bring him in."

"How come?"

"Soon as he saw what he was getting into, he got understandably nervous."

"He and that redhead were all over each other."

Franklin burst into a new round of laughter. "That was his favorite bird. They ran up a dinner tab of fifty-nine quid!"

"That's a bigger bill than *I* had," Mark said, "And I had *two* companions."

"Not only that, Mark, but the British taxpayer is picking up Edgar's whole night on the town. He's already put it on his expense sheet!"

"Well," Mark said, "I'm just glad to be getting a breather. I might make a trip to the States. I need to cover my ass with the optical company I'm *supposed* to be working for. Now it's up to you guys."

"If I can make progress," Jim said, "Mark will probably have to come back into it."

Once again they went over the thorny question of the £1500 payment being demanded by the counterfeiters and yet stubbornly being withheld by the Yard. "There's still a lot of cynicism," Franklin said. "The feeling is that the printer is too smart to be sussed out even if we did give you the dough."

"What do *you* think?" Mark asked.

"I think," Franklin said, "that we should have one more round."

"Hello?"

"Brad?"

"Speaking."

"It's Lee. Did he give you the money last night?"

"There's a slight technical problem still in the way."

"He failed to make the payment?"

"Yes, but—"

"Well, Brad, that's too bad. What's his excuse this time?"

"He has to be convinced that we have the full amount."

"Did he see the serial numbers?"

"Yes, but—"

"Then he must *know* I've got the quantity. It should be obvious to him."

"He says his people want proof."

"The numbers are proof enough. It means I have thirty different printings at least! Does he think I'm an amateur?"

"No, hardly that."

"Okay, so you just drop it. I'm sorry, but it's off."

"He says he'll pay if his minder can see the big bulk."

"The brother-in-law?"

"Right."

"He's a Scotsman?"

"Yes."

"Well, he's probably with the Yard."

"I don't know, Lee."

"You certainly put a lot of trust in them, but they can't have much faith in you."

"The American wants us to bring in the minder blindfolded, then let him look at the bulk."

"I'd have to arrange for people to bring it somewhere. I'd need two minders of my own for that. But there's nobody I trust."

"Nobody?"

"Maybe you don't realize what money does to small-time crooks. If they see ninety-five thousand pounds of what I've got, they'll blow their bottle."

"I could take the stuff somewhere and my man Ron would bring in the Scotsman."

"No, no, no. You're too exposed already."

"I feel strongly that he's on the level."

"Brad, it could be a setup."

"But the man is willing to pay just as soon as he's convinced we have the rest! He's all set!"

"I know you're irritated with me, but all I can say is that obviously they don't trust you. You can't even make them believe the truth. Why do *you* believe everything *they* say?"

"I've spent time with the American. He's told me about his organization. He's got—"

"Brad, you've dropped them five thousand pounds of my work and what have they done? They haven't paid a penny yet."

"The man operates at a higher level. He doesn't bother with—"

"Cut out the personalities, forget the personalities. You're the salesman, not me. If you can't convince him, that's up to you. Stop telling me how he's such a great guy and how much money he's got. Don't be swayed, because we've seen nothing back yet. If he won't pay, tell him to return the load he's got."

"I wish we could find a way to proceed with the man."

"Brad, if he's genuine, let him give the load back to you.

We can do something with him another time."

"Look, if you want to meet him—"

Before Brad could finish his sentence, he heard the Magician laugh and then the silence of the dead phone line.

Later in the afternoon, Brad conferred with Ron at the taxi garage. He reported the printer's anger over Mark's demand for further proof that the additional notes existed. And, he went on, the plan to have Jim brought in blindfolded was unworkable.

Ron swore up and down in frustration. He wasn't sure which man to blame, Mark or the Magician. "We're too close to let it go now," he said. The two men discussed various possible ways of letting Jim see the balance of the notes, but none seemed feasible until Ron suggested that they take a photograph of the bills and show it to Jim. With renewed enthusiasm, they called Mark's house. When Jim answered, Ron proposed a meeting for the following morning at eleven o'clock, again at the Carlton Tower Hotel.

"I'll be there," Jim said, "but Mark is waiting until he can meet with the printer."

"I understand," Ron replied. He hung up and turned to Brad. "The meet is on with Jim," he said.

"The Magician thinks Jim is the Yard," Brad said. "And he feels Mark is the FBI."

Ron exploded in anger all over again. He told Brad to leave that to him. He, Ron, knew coppers when he saw them. Once they got Jim alone, it would be easy to authenticate him.

Thursday,
17 October

In the morning at New Scotland Yard, Jim was "wired up" for the first time in his career. A small tape recorder, not much larger than a pack of cigarettes, was strapped to his left side. A thin wire led from the machine to his chest and through his shirt, to a tiny microphone clipped to the back of his tie. He knew the danger in carrying such equipment, but the Yard wanted to start getting the counterfeit-money dealers' words on tape.

Jim still expected to be blindfolded and taken to an unknown place, where he would be given a quick glimpse of £95,000 worth of forged currency. Perhaps the recorder would pick up sounds that would identify the location.

Tasty Miller and the other detectives wished Jim luck and he set off. It had been a gray morning, but now the sun was breaking through as he drove into Knightsbridge and parked outside 20 Wilton Place. It was ten o'clock, giving him an hour to prepare for the meeting at the Carlton Tower.

In the house, he joined Mark and Monica at the dining-room table and lit a cigarette. Jim was a "social" smoker, being able to smoke without making it a habit, but this morning he puffed on one weed after another and drank his fifth, sixth, and seventh cups of coffee. Over the past few weeks, his consumption of coffee and cigarettes had been far greater than ever in his life; and now, with the added tension of knowing that he was about to go off alone, secretly wired with a recorder, he felt a steadily growing nausea.

131

"You look pale," Monica said.

"Well, I'm not feeling all that clever this morning."

Mark smiled at him and said, "Just as long as you *act* clever, me lad. This job is a wee bit tasty, remember?"

He sat in the rear of the Carlton Tower's mezzanine-floor lounge, sipping more coffee and smoking, when he saw Brad and Ron coming toward him. Jim quickly reached around to his side and pressed the "start" button on the tape recorder. The three men exchanged some chit-chat while the waitress took more coffee orders. When she had gone, Brad reported that the Magician would not allow Jim to see the balance of the forged notes.

"What's the matter with him?" Jim asked out of genuine disappointment. "Doesn't he trust us?"

"He trusts you going in to see it," Brad said, "but it would mean him having to arrange for the notes to be taken somewhere and looked after by a couple of blokes."

"Two minders," Ron echoed.

Jim puffed on his cigarette. "I can see it means bringing other people into it," he said, "but try and look at it from our point of view. We can't move forward until we satisfy ourselves that there's more to come from your side."

Brad and Ron started talking at once, explaining how they had come up with the idea of photographing the £95,000 worth of forged notes and using the picture as proof of their existence. Jim instantly agreed. Brad also said he would put some sort of object on top of the counterfeit bills and *then* take the photograph, to prove it was current.

"Fine," Jim said.

"I'll speak to the printer," Brad said, "and then I'll ring you at Mark's to arrange a meeting."

"At that meeting you'll have the photograph?"

"Absolutely," Brad said. "And you'll have the fifteen hundred pounds?"

Jim hesitated, realizing that he was rapidly running out of options. "Of course I'll have it," he said.

"Until we have that first payment for what we've already delivered," Brad persisted, "the entire deal is held up."

Ron cocked his head to one side. "I'll tell you what's happened on this thing," he said, shaking his finger. "It's all Mark's fault! He's been fucking it up! He's a bullshitter! He won't pay!"

"Wait a minute," Jim said. "You can't expect us to throw money away. If your photograph shows you've got the quantity we want, the deal will go ahead."

Brad remained calm, staring at Jim as if to test his reactions. "It'll never go ahead unless you pay for the first load," he said evenly. "Do you understand why?"

Jim stared back at him. "I think so, yes."

"The reason," Brad continued, "is because otherwise the man thinks it's a setup."

Jim forced a smile "You mean that what we're offering is too good for him to be true?"

"We mean," Ron countered, "that we've investigated Mark."

"You have?"

"We fucking-bloody-well have," Ron said.

Brad held up his hand for his associate to keep quiet. "We thought he might have been an FBI agent."

Jim inhaled, then let out a thin stream of smoke. His stomach felt worse than ever. "That will amuse Mark when I tell him," he said in the most cheerful manner possible. Looking around, he noticed that the coffee lounge had filled up with participants from a seminar being held in the ballroom on the same floor. "Let's take a drive," he suggested. "If you don't mind, I'd like some fresh air."

"All right," Brad said. "We'll take a ride in the park. Ron, why don't you get us a cab?"

"Sure, mate."

When Ron had gone, Jim and Brad sipped their coffee in silence. Brad said, "The thing is, Jim, the man expected me to come back with the money after we had dinner with Mark the other night. He's angry. What's more, he can't understand why you don't believe he's got the rest of the notes. He says it should be obvious."

"Obvious to him, but not to us."

"I tried to tell him that. But he wonders why you don't have more faith in what I'm telling you. Especially after you've seen the serial numbers."

"We do have faith in you, Brad, but we know that you're not calling the tune on this deal. And that's the problem."

"I asked the man if he'd meet with Mark, but he just laughed."

Jim shrugged. "For someone as cautious as this man is, he's in the wrong business."

"He feels that if there's going to be any risk at all, it's not worth it."

"But we're trying to make sure there's as little risk as possible—to make it safe for everyone!"

"I'm telling you, Jim, there isn't enough money in the whole of this world to catch him. He's got it set up so there's no weak link. There's only himself to blame if he goes under."

"With us," Jim said, "he couldn't be any safer. The reason he's being so pigheaded is that he doesn't realize what Mark's family is all about. He doesn't grasp what kind of people we have behind us. The only reason we're still in this game is because we recognize his genius. He's produced a five-pound note that we think it's worth our while to persevere with."

"He also wants to get on with his ten-pound note," Brad said.

"He's got good inside information. I'll give him credit there."

"He's brilliant."

"Well, Brad, if he doesn't trust you, we've no hope of pulling this deal off."

"I know," Brad said.

"He should realize what the family means."

"Yes," Brad agreed. "He should realize about the family."

As they walked downstairs to the lobby, Jim was not only sick to his stomach but sweating and suffering hot-and-cold flashes. He slipped a hand under his jacket and managed to switch off the recorder, to preserve as much tape as he could.

Outside, Ron was standing next to a taxicab parked at the curb. Jim tipped the hotel doorman as he climbed in back with the two men. Brad sat to his left and Ron pulled down the cricket seat facing him. The driver pulled away and headed in the direction of Hyde Park.

"We can talk in here," Ron said. "He can't hear anything, 'cause I've closed the windows tight." He indicated the glass shield separating them from the driver. "We'll go for a spin around the park and then we can drop you anywhere you like."

Moving as if to adjust his legs, Jim reached around and turned on his tape recorder. He tried to avoid thinking about the condition of his stomach, although he felt increasingly as if he were about to vomit. I'm not going to be sick, he told himself, repeating the vow in his mind as the cab jostled his insides.

"This deal makes or breaks me with the printer," Brad said. "If I bollix it up, he can say it was all my fault."

"When can you get in touch with him again?" Jim asked.

"That's up to him."

"Will he do the big deal, do you think?"

"If you get me the bloody fifteen hundred pounds, I think I can convince him. When I met Mark, I thought, Great, we've got someone with all these outlets. See, I could move up to the top floor on the printer's level, as his partner."

"Me, too," Ron said.

"That's what I've wanted," Brad went on. "But I've got to keep the Magician sweet, because at any time he can cut me off."

"So," Jim said, "it's up to you to convince him."

"Once I take the money to him, there'll be no problem. The fifteen hundred pounds has held it up all this time. The money will give the printer some faith."

"That's the truth," Ron said.

Brad indicated a gold ring on his finger. "When we photograph the notes, I'll put this on top of 'em, to prove the picture is current. Will that satisfy you?"

"It should, Brad. I see no problem . . ." Jim's voice trailed off as he bent over, holding his stomach. By now they were riding through Hyde Park and he was feeling so ill that he could hardly talk.

"What's the matter?" Ron asked.

"You'll have to excuse me," Jim said in a weak voice. "I think I'm going to be sick. You'll have to stop the cab. . . ."

Ron slid open the glass partition and yelled to the driver to pull over at Bayswater Road bordering the northern edge of the park. "Hang on, Old Jim, don't let 'er spill in here."

"Had a late-night meal," Jim whispered, making up a story. "It was full of rich food. . . . Haven't felt well . . . all morning. . . . Got to leave cab. . . ."

"Here we go," Ron said as the taxicab pulled to the curb. Jim had to cross to his left, in order to get out on the sidewalk. Brad put out a hand to help him—and Jim felt it land on the tape recorder. In shock, the two men stared at each other. Brad yanked his hand away and recoiled, apparently assuming that the object under Jim's coat was a gun.

Sweating from sickness and fear, Jim felt himself roll out of the cab, stagger across the sidewalk, and drop to his knees on the grass. He was dizzy and about to heave, but now both Brad and Ron were out of the cab, offering to help him.

"Just leave me here," Jim groaned. "I'm feeling a bit better. I'll get another cab on my own." He stared up at the two men and added, "You don't really think Mark is an FBI agent, do you?"

Ron put a hand on Jim's shoulder and bent down, speaking directly into the microphone behind the tie. "Jim, you rest on me, boy. I can smell the Old Bill a mile away."

At his taxicab office in the East End, Brad was checking the drivers' trip sheets when the phone rang. It was Lee. "How's the weather?" he asked.

"The Scotsman will have the money," Brad replied.

"I thought I told you to get out of that."

"I know," Brad said, "but every instinct I have tells me they're on the level. All they want is a photograph."

"Photograph?"

"Yes—to give him proof that we have the quantity they

want. That will avoid you having to hire some minders."

"Well, I suppose we could do that."

Brad felt an enormous sense of relief. "Great," he said. "But first, just see if he brings the money."

"Why? He won't give it to me unless I have the photograph!"

"Brad, you'll just have to do things the way I tell you. If he brings the money, tell him you'll show it to me. Once I see it, you'll bring the photograph he wants. But he has to let the cash out of his hands first. Do you understand why?"

"Because—"

"Because, Brad, he could be the Old Bill. And the Yank—who knows?"

"But he's carrying a gun, sir."

"You saw it?"

Brad hesitated. He was sure that the object he had felt under Jim's coat had been a small pistol. "Yes," he lied. "I saw it. If he was the Yard, he wouldn't be armed."

"Well, the point is that he'd be forbidden to give you any cash."

"So I should still call his bluff?"

"Of course. After all, what you're asking him is quite reasonable. Once he pays for what he's got, we'll show him the photograph and possibly negotiate a larger deal. Just tell him what I said. But ring him from a pay phone."

"Why?"

"Because there may be a tap on your line."

"You think so?"

"Yes, but don't worry. And from now on, I think it wise if you and I communicate only in person."

"Okay," Brad said, his heart pounding.

"First, just get the money. That's the good faith you need. When I call, let me know if you have it by saying,

'See you at the racetrack,' and I'll explain what to do. Got that?"

"Got it," Brad said, remembering how Lee had once told him that he often frequented the Catford Dog Track. Once again Brad was torn between his suspicions and his desire to do business with Mark. By now his future with the Magician hinged on this deal.

He went out to a pay phone and rang Mark's number. When Monica answered, he said, "May I speak to your brother, please?" There was a slight hesitation, but in a few moments Jim came on the line. Brad reported that he'd spoken to "the man" and that everything looked good.

"What about the photograph?" Jim asked.

Brad answered, "I have clearance for it," which was true as far as it went. He avoided mentioning that he'd be able to get it only *after* the forger saw the £1500. "Do you have the money?" he asked.

"It's being put together," Jim answered, "but it might take a few days to get untraceable bills."

They agreed to meet on Monday morning. Brad suggested that Jim wait outside the Piccadilly entrance of the Park Lane Hotel.

"Ron and I will pick you up," he said.

Friday,
18 October

Jim showed up early at the Yard to try and persuade Superintendent Miller to release the necessary cash. It was imperative, he argued, if he were to make any further progress in getting to the Magician. Everything hung by that slender thread.

He was at his desk when he looked up and saw Commander Harold Grant approaching. The senior police officer had charge of the entire D.5/2 investigation, of which Operation Wellington was only a part. Although Jim was merely a young detective constable, his athletic stature was well-known to Grant and other superiors.

"How's the case going?" the commander asked.

"Sir, I really feel that if we persevere we'll get the forger."

"Do you trust this Yarry chap?"

"Yes, I do. But right now our hands are tied."

Grant nodded and wandered off. Within an hour, to Jim's surprise, Superintendent Miller called him in and asked if a meeting could be arranged between Commander Grant and Mark. As Miller explained it, there was some concern that Mark would go to the newspapers and unleash his frustrations. Perhaps the commander could appease him.

Mark was scheduled to fly back to the States in the evening. He had appointments with executives of the optical-import firm in Connecticut and hoped to bolster their trust in him. The company was hugely successful in having eyeglasses frames manufactured according to its own specifications in Japan, Korea, and France, then distributing the products in the United States. Mark, in turn, had made inroads for distribution in Europe. His goal had been to line up at least $250,000 worth of orders in the first month, but so far he had fallen short. He would have to explain, without revealing the details, that he had been "slightly distracted" over the past four weeks. He would have to convince the company's owners that the expense of his Knightsbridge home was justified; and that perhaps in a few more months, by Christmas, the European headquarters would be in full swing. Losing the job would not be overwhelming, but Mark hated to fail at something by not making his best efforts.

He felt it might be worth everything, however, if the Magician were caught. So far, the experience had been one of total frustration. He had always had a high regard for Scotland Yard; but up close, this powerful institution with its magnificent reputation seemed far less impressive.

He agreed to meet with Commander Grant, but not with any great hope of persuading him to release the £1500. Mark was accustomed to viewing such obstacles as only minor problems in comparison to the goal to be achieved; but, as before, he steeled himself against providing the all-important payment out of his own pocket. It could endanger Jim's career by being used as evidence that he had "lost control" of the operation. Beyond that, Mark was not about to help the Yard out of its own inflexibility. If the police wanted to hamper and even kill the case, that was their problem, not his.

Furthermore, in the past few days Mark had begun to concentrate more on his roles as husband and father. He was grateful to Monica for having been so understanding up to this point, but it was difficult for her to avoid resenting the constant invasion of her privacy. With Jim Goldie on hand up to twenty hours a day, the household could hardly be called her own. She would be glad to see the end of "this little adventure," as Mark had described it to her.

Monica hadn't regarded it as a serious matter. In the earliest stages, she hadn't even cared to discuss it; but when events escalated, she began to join the conversations over lunch and dinner. By now she knew the basics of the case and could identify the characters. But she was also determined to stay in the background. She dealt with the housekeeper and the nanny, attended to the children, and went on with her own life. Much of her time and energy were spent as president of the London Chapter of World Wings, the association of former Pan Am flight attendants.

She had developed an attitude, from having lived with Mark nearly nine years, that almost anything could be expected; and so the extraordinary had become normal. Mark liked to joke that if he were to come home tugging an elephant through the door, Monica would simply shrug and ask, "What kind of peanuts does he eat?" In that context, serving coffee or tea to members of a counterfeiting ring, and having a Scotland Yard detective in the house around the clock, could hardly faze her.

For Mark, the rendezvous with Commander Grant was mostly an annoyance; but as he left the house by cab this afternoon, he leaned his head back and tried to summon up an image of the Magician. What would it be like to meet him in person? To try and lure such a brilliant, cautious man into a trap? By the time the taxicab reached its destination, Mark was caught up in the whole adventure all over again.

The meeting place was a block of modern, west-end apartments near the Vauxhall Bridge. There was a large indoor swimming pool, a set of tennis courts, and a restaurant. Mark joined Commander Grant at a corner table overlooking the pool.

It felt as if at last he had come face-to-face with a character straight out of a British thriller. Grant was a large, powerful-looking man with a dry, confident manner. The father figure of them all, Mark thought.

"Mr. Yarry," Grant said over tea, "you know that this is a serious matter under investigation."

"Certainly."

"It involves, in perhaps more ways than one, the security of the country."

"I understand."

"Now, the requests you are making—"

"You mean the money we need?"

"Yes—it may seem quite reasonable and simple to you, but it's not so simple for the Government."

"You know that I asked for one small piece of bank-note paper?"

"I'm afraid we couldn't do that."

"Okay," Mark said, "but I'm only trying to do the job."

"I appreciate that," Grant said. "Now, if by some good fortune the case reaches another level, would you continue your involvement?"

"Well, that depends."

"We can't force you. But if you walk out entirely, it might not go so well for us. You understand, Mr. Yarry, that you are in a position of some power?"

Mark nodded slightly, trying to size up this man who seemed like a general who had finally come to the front line. For nearly two hours, the two men tried to take each other's measure. The conversation was polite and respectful. Through it all, Mark instinctively allowed Grant to gain the upper hand and to feel that he, Mark, could be trusted. That was what Grant wanted to see in the mirror, so that was the image Mark reflected. By the end of the meeting, Commander Grant had agreed to go to a still-higher authority, to Deputy Assistant Commissioner Ernest Bond. No promises were made, but there was mutual respect and, perhaps, a breakthrough.

In the evening, Mark flew to the States as planned; at the same time, Jim Goldie received word that a special squad within the Yard would supply the £1500 sometime the following week. When he hung up the phone, Jim poured himself a drink and wondered how Mark had accomplished the impossible. It would be the first time Scotland Yard had ever parted with money to make a counterfeit buy.

Monday,
21 October

In the morning, Jim strapped on his tape recorder and microphone in preparation for the meeting with Brad and Ron. At about ten o'clock, Sergeant Franklin dropped over to say that the Yard had set up a special telephone, manned by an agent who would answer calls posing as a member of Mark's fictitious organization. Jim was to give the forged-currency dealers this special phone number, which could not be traced, and ask them to use it whenever they wanted to be in touch with him.

But there was another matter, of much more importance, that Lurch Franklin had come to discuss. The £1500 would be arranged in packages of £10 notes and Franklin himself would bring the money to Jim tomorrow evening. Therefore, Jim could promise Brad and Ron with certainty that he would have it by Wednesday morning. There was a catch, however: Jim would have to make every effort to prevent the money from leaving his possession. He could show it to them, and let them count each bill if they liked, but he must hold on to the Yard's cash if at all possible.

As he drove toward the Park Lane Hotel, Jim tried to retain a positive frame of mind despite the crippling instruction. His immediate job was to stall Brad and Ron for two more days; and to do that, he would have to project total optimism and confidence. They were expecting the money this morning, so their disappointment would be acute. If pushed too far, an exasperated Ron Schneider might even turn violent. It would be necessary to come on strong at the outset.

Jim parked his car on a side street and walked the several blocks east on Piccadilly until he came to the hotel. It was about two minutes before eleven o'clock. He waited outside the entrance, his hidden recorder already running, and he stared across the street toward Green Park. At exactly eleven, a taxicab pulled up to the curb next to him. Ron was driving and Brad, in the backseat, gestured for Jim to get in. When he did, Ron stepped on the gas and sped off.

"Got the photograph?" Jim asked.

"I can have it taken today," Brad said. "If you have the money, we'll be in business."

"I'll have it Wednesday morning."

"What? Jesus, man—"

"Hey, Jim," said Ron, who was driving rather wildly, "what the hell is this all about?"

"Mark is out of the U.K. on business," Jim said. "His signature is required on the check, but he's due back tomorrow. He just concluded a big deal for the organization, so they're celebrating. But I'll get the cash tomorrow afternoon and we can meet back here Wednesday morning."

Brad, seated to his right, glanced at him with an expression of weariness and pain. "I'm disappointed," he mumbled. "I was all keyed up to go ahead today."

"You're stabbing us in the heart, old Jim," said Ron as he made a sudden, violent U-turn that sent Jim and Brad reeling to one side.

"Look," Jim said, "here's how serious I am." He handed Brad a slip of paper on which he had written, "P.M. Associates—737-2426—Mr. Cameron." The company name was fictitious, but the number was for the authentic phone that the Yard had installed somewhere in the suburbs of London. Jim had borrowed the name "Cameron" from Mark's ballooning colleague, Don Cameron. "That's one of the family's places here in England," he said. "I'm trusting you with the number."

"Who is Mr. Cameron?"

"That's my alias. Just ask for Mr. Cameron and I'll get word. Giving you this information is my way of showing you I mean business. If I didn't expect good things to happen, I'd never give you that piece of paper."

Brad studied it. "This is Mark's organization?"

"It's just one of our companies. We've put a lot of money into legitimate business."

"I understand," Brad said.

"So call me there tomorrow if you like. I'll confirm our appointment for the following day."

"All right," Brad said. "But I'm still disappointed."

They were driving through Hyde Park. Ron stopped the cab near the Serpentine, the long crescent of water running from Kensington Gardens through the center of the park's main grounds. To compensate for having to keep Brad and Ron waiting two more days, and to inject a sense of momentum into the meeting, Jim decided to make a major concession.

"Listen," he said, "instead of a hundred thousand pounds in forged notes, we'll accept a deal for fifty grand. Then we'll do a second transaction the same size. Each time, we'll pay you fifteen thousand pounds in cash."

"That's terrific," Brad said. "The printer might go for it."

"You just tell him that's the minimum amount we'll accept. If he doesn't agree, there's no deal."

"I'll give him the message," Brad said. "But first, you'll

have the fifteen hundred pounds on Wednesday morning?"

"That's right."

"Because I need it to show him. Then I can get your photograph and we're all set for the rest of the deal."

"After the fifteen hundred is paid, I'll have thirteen thousand five hundred pounds to pay for a balance of forty-five grand from you."

Ron poked his head through the opening of the cab's glass partition. "Jim, boy," he said, "now you're talking sense."

"Hello."

"Good afternoon, Brad. Have you got any news?"

"No news," Brad said, referring to the fact that he still did not have the first payment. "But we're meeting again—"

At the other end, Lee hung up. Brad held the phone to his ear. He had wanted to tell the Magician to ring back on Wednesday afternoon, for some "news" at last. He had wanted to convey the positive side of things.

Tuesday, 22 October

The officer assigned to the Yard's special phone in the London suburbs picked it up on the first ring. "P.M. Associates. May I help you?"

"Can I speak to Mr. Cameron?"

"He's not here, but I can take a message."

"I want to confirm our appointment for tomorrow morning."

"Who is speaking?"

"Brad."

"Mr. Cameron left word for you. The appointment is confirmed."

"Thank you," Brad said.

"You're quite welcome," the officer replied.

Wednesday, 23 October

Switching on his tape recorder, Jim Goldie stood at the Piccadilly entrance of the Park Lane Hotel and waited. This time he was wearing a suede safari jacket over an open-neck shirt, with a medallion on a chain hanging down over the top of his chest. The recorder was strapped to his side again and the tiny microphone was clipped onto the chain, concealed by the medallion. If Brad asked him outright whether he was carrying a gun, it would be a difficult moment. Jim could answer truthfully that he was not armed, but Brad might ask, "Then what is that object under your jacket?" If Jim said he *was* carrying a gun, Brad could ask to see it. In either case, there was jeopardy; and now Jim sensed the strong possibility that "being wired" was a fatal mistake. Well, he thought, it's too late now.

Clutched in his right hand, attached by handcuffs to his wrist, was the "security" briefcase which Sergeant Franklin had delivered to his home the night before. It held a total of one hundred and fifty genuine £10 notes from Scotland Yard. Each of three sealed, cellophane bank bags contained fifty "tenners" or £500.

Jim was intrigued by the thought that passers-by streaming in and out of the hotel could have no idea that he was a detective constable carrying the first actual "buy money" in the Yard's history. There was hardly any way to avoid giving it over to Brad and Ron; but he would have to release the £1500 only after a demonstration of great reluctance, to make them feel as if taking possession of it was a monumental victory. He would also have to unnerve them by referring to the power of Mark's organization to retaliate if anything went wrong with the rest of the deal. If the Yard were to lose this cash without being able to arrest *anyone*, Jim's future as a detective would be dim.

Still no sign of the counterfeit-money contacts. Perhaps they had already figured out that he was the Old Bill and were setting a trap for him. Just in case, Sergeant Franklin was waiting in Hyde Park, dressed in overalls and posing as a gardener pruning branches and raking leaves. If Jim could guide Brad and Ron to drive into the park, at least there would be some assitance in the event of trouble.

Brad and Ron were in a taxicab at the opposite side of the Park Lane Hotel. For the past fifteen minutes, they had been debating whether to go ahead with the meeting. The prospect of actually receiving £1500 from Jim had forced them into a state of extreme alertness. If the "big Scotch geezer" really was from the Yard, he would have to arrest them as soon as they tried to go off with the genuine cash.

"We don't know for sure that he's not the Old Bill," Ron said.

"The question is whether we take the chance," Brad replied.

The two men sat there nervously trying to reassure each other that Jim was not, after all, a police officer. "At least we're clean right now," Ron said with a sigh. "And he's got no choice but to give us the money. If he doesn't, that's the end. Clear and simple."

Jim's tape machine recorded the traffic noise from the front of the Park Lane Hotel, then the sound of Ron

Schneider's footsteps and his cockney-accented greeting: "We gotta come 'round this way, 'cause the traffic's bleeding solid."

JIM: Well, I got the stuff.
RON: Ah, yes. Good.
(Jim followed him back through the hotel and outside to the rear parking area. While Ron jumped into the driver's seat of the cab, Jim got into the back with Brad, who immediately spied the briefcase.)
BRAD: You've got it.
JIM (*opening the briefcase to show* BRAD *the three bags of £10 notes*): Got the money.
BRAD: Good. That's the first part of the deal over with. Why not leave it with us and we'll talk tomorrow?
JIM: Ah, well, let's have a drive in the park.
BRAD: If you want, Jim.
(Ron started the motor and drove off.)
JIM: Have you spoken to the man?
BRAD: Not yet. I won't speak to him till I can go back with the collateral. As far as he's concerned, this is the first deal. Now it's completed. It should have been done before now. I can go to him this time and say, "Well, here's the money. Now this is what else we want to do." If anything goes boss-eyed, I'll exchange the money back to you for the notes we delivered.
JIM: Good enough.
BRAD: That's the only way I can work it. I've got to go back with concrete.
JIM: I want you to count it before you take it.
BRAD: As long as there's fifteen. Fifteen hundred pounds, that's all.
JIM: Just want you to be sure.
BRAD: You've got the okay for the balance?
JIM: Yep.
BRAD: That's all I wanted to know.
(As the cab headed into Hyde Park, the two agreed to a deadline

150

of Monday—five days from now—for the transaction. By that time, Brad would have an additional £45,000 in forged notes from the printer; and Jim would have £13,500 in cash to complete his first payment.)

BRAD: Now, about the photograph—if you want to show up with the rest of the money, I'll have the stuff, so there's not much point in fucking about with photographs, is there?

JIM: Brad, don't try to screw me.

BRAD: I'm just thinking time-wise. But it's up to you.

JIM: You mean once he sees this money here, there shouldn't be any complications?

BRAD: There shouldn't be, Jim. He'll say, "You can carry on, Brad. Make the deal as you want to do it."

JIM: Why can't we do it Friday?

BRAD: I may need the extra couple of days over the weekend. That's the only reason. I want to be sure to make contact with him and set it all up.

JIM: Let's meet Friday anyway. You bring this money back and show me you still have it. I'll have the other cash from my end, too.

BRAD: Well, okay—

JIM: And the transaction is maybe Friday but Monday for sure.

BRAD: That's it, Jim. That's good. There's no problem with Monday.

JIM: I hope there won't be.

BRAD: I wish this had all been done at the beginning. Fifteen hundred was the key to it.

JIM (raising his voice to be heard): Ron, when you can find a place to stop, I want you both to count this money before I give it to you.

RON: Just making sure we've got no tails on us. Know what I mean, Jim?

JIM: Fine.

BRAD: Go down toward the pond.

(The taxicab stopped in Kensington Gardens. Jim Goldie's recorder kept running. The tape picked up the loud crackling noise of Brad Lewis tearing open one of the cellophane bags. But

Ron Schneider turned around in the driver's seat and injected a new note into the proceedings.)

RON: Jim, are you Mark's brother-in-law?

JIM (*without hesitation*): No.

RON: You don't half look like his wife. That's what made me wonder. You're not his brother-in-law?

BRAD (*busily counting*): Come in the back with us, Ron. (*To JIM*) What are these, fives and tens?

JIM: All tens.

BRAD (*counting*): One, two, three . . .

(Anxious to get his hands on the money, too, Ron jumped out of the cab. But he stood outside, looking all around.)

RON: Just making sure we've not been tailed here. . . .

BRAD: . . . eleven, twelve . . .

JIM (*opening the rear door*): Come on in, Ron, and make yourself busy.

RON (*to BRAD, while still debating with himself over whether to climb into the back*): Wouldn't it be better if we did this while driving along? (*After getting a negative headshake from BRAD*) No?

JIM: It won't take two minutes to count it.

RON (*referring to the three bags of cash*): What are they, monkeys?

JIM (*responding, even though the term "monkey," in reference to a packet of £500, was a cockney expression*): Yeah, three monkeys.

BRAD: . . . twenty-two, twenty-three . . .

RON: Fifty tenners in each bag, eh?

JIM: Right. Come on in.

RON: Well, if it's no deal on Monday you'll get it all back Jim. Just give us the five grand we dropped with Mark, and we're even. (*Getting into the rear of the cab as he grabs a "monkey"*) How do you open these bags?

JIM: Just rip 'em apart.

BRAD: Rip it open.

(At this point, Jim declared that he was going to "hold on to" £500. They could have £1000, he said, but he would keep the

152

remaining "monkey" until they entered the larger transaction, for which this was a mere down payment.)

JIM: If your man wants to see some money, a grand is sufficient.

RON: Oh, Jim boy!

BRAD: All he's getting back is the first deal that he done, Jim! He's sold some gear, right? You've got the gear still, as collateral.

JIM: So take him a thousand quid.

RON: Well, he wants fifteen hundred! (*To* BRAD) That's one monkey, there.

BRAD: Jim, I don't want to take just a grand. To be quite honest—

JIM: Well, that's it, then.

RON (*desperately*): What's the difference between a grand and fifteen hundred, Jim? What's a bloody monkey? Don't hold back on us, boy!

JIM: Ron, we have been fucked about from asshole to breakfast time on this deal.

RON: No, it's Mark who's done the fucking about!

JIM: Take a thousand—

RON: You've had five grand for a fortnight now of our money, old boy.

JIM: I should think it's a load of shit, anyway. Not qualitywise, but from the firm's point of view, the amount is shit. (Jim and Ron argued back and forth over how much the £5000 in forged notes could be "changed-up" on the illegal market. Jim made the point that Mark had "no interest whatsoever" in disposing of such a small quantity, so that this initial deal was "worthless" by itself; and then he sat back and calmly repeated that all they could have was £1000.)

BRAD: Fifteen hundred, Jim! I can't go back to the Magician with less!

JIM: What's that going to prove to him?

BRAD: That you've done the deal!

JIM: We haven't done the fucking about, it's the printer. He's forced you to make promises you couldn't keep.

BRAD: I've told you the truth from the beginning.

JIM: All right, you've been honest. We appreciate that. But you're not calling the tune on this. It's your man. The printer's the bloke that's holding everything up.

BRAD: If he sees this payment and still says no on the bigger deal, I'll bring it back to you.

JIM: I'm getting together the balance (*referring to the £13,500*) for Friday.

BRAD: Okay, but from my end I'm promising only for Monday.

JIM: At least bring the photograph on Friday, then. If your man promises to supply us regularly, we'll pay a hundred and fifty points for the first transaction. One pound fifty per bill.

RON: Per bill, yeah.

JIM: For ten thousand pieces, he's getting fifteen thousand pounds. If he wants to double that, we'll give you thirty grand. We'll pay that price on *any* amount, for the first deal. But after that, a hundred and fifty points is too much.

BRAD: We haven't even settled up for *this* stinking deal yet, so how can we talk to him about the future?

RON: Jim, he's right. You've gotta settle up for the pieces you got. How else can we go ahead?

BRAD: We can't!

RON: We'll be here on Friday. We've never let you down on a meet yet.

(By this time, Jim had created such desperation in Brad and Ron that they repeatedly gave assurances that the full transaction would happen by Monday or Jim would have his £1500 back—if only he would give it to them now, in full!)

JIM: Ron, whatever happens, you'll be taken care of by the family.

RON: By Mark's family?

JIM: Right. And even ol' Dave (*the first taxicab driver*) will probably get a bonus out of it as well. Mark's people are very generous when they're treated right.

RON: Well, we don't know anything about Dave. He's on the missing list.

154

BRAD: Jim, your last word to me was that you had fifteen hundred.

JIM: And here it is.

BRAD: Can I take it to the man?

JIM: Will he give us nine thousand pieces more?

BRAD: I hope so, Jim.

JIM: Will he trust you with thirteen-five from me? Trust that you'll get it to him safely?

BRAD: Oh, yeah. And we get our cut.

JIM: All he's given us so far is bits of paper. What I'm giving you is real. I'm parting with it. But you might not even turn up on Friday.

RON: Jim, don't be daft.

JIM: Why can't you accept one grand against the full fifteen grand?

RON: Jim, don't hold back a monkey on us!

BRAD: A fucking five hundred pounds, Jim!

(At just the right psychological moment, Jim switched the conversation abruptly.)

JIM: Brad, have you checked out Mark's family?

BRAD: Why?

JIM: Well, we've checked you out.

BRAD: Yes?

JIM: That's right, *Mr. Lewis.*

(It was the first time that Brad's last name had been mentioned. He stared back as if he had just received a blow to the stomach.)

BRAD: You checked me out?

JIM: Of course.

BRAD: So you know all about me. Then you must know the printer wants this fifteen hundred in full.

JIM: Is he so narrow-minded that an extra monkey's gonna make all the difference?

RON: Yes, that's the truth!

JIM: He wants it done this way only, huh?

RON: That's it, Jim. His way or not at all. Definitely! But what's a monkey to Mark's people if they're supposed to be such big businessmen?

JIM: You'd better believe they are, Ron.

155

RON: Well, truly I do believe it. But by the same rule, why so long for a poxy fifteen hundred pounds? That's a polish, ain't it? To a slag it might be a fortune, but—

BRAD: Jim, the point is that the man just doesn't trust you! (After more bickering, created almost entirely by Jim's calculated reluctance to part with the full amount of money in his briefcase, he agreed at last to do so. He reiterated that the price of £1.50 per note would have to be renegotiated after the first deal was completed.)

JIM: After that, there's got to be a reduction in points paid per bill.

RON: Look, Jim, don't strangle us, boy. We gotta live, you know. What with the printer strangling us and you strangling us, we've got a kick up the ballocks to nothing.

JIM: We're going to be giving your man regular business. We could be the only outlet he'd ever need.

RON: I couldn't agree more.

JIM: All the problems off his hands.

BRAD: It's a point I'll hammer home to him.

JIM: And remember, we haven't even met the bloke. But if we're doing business with both of you, for the entire future, that suits us fine.

RON: 'Atta boy, Jim.

JIM: Now, when I hand you thirteen-five on Friday or Monday, is he going to pick it up himself?

BRAD: No, no. I deliver it to him alone.

JIM: If you take off with our money, and the printer comes bleating to Mark . . .

RON: No fear of that, Jim.

BRAD: Yeah, no fear of me fucking running away with it.

JIM: Okay, so take the fifteen hundred quid. I trust you. (When Brad had stuffed the cash into his pockets, Ron suddenly remembered his suspicions.)

RON: Now, Jim, you've done some checking on us. Right? And I've asked you if you're Mark's brother-in-law. You said no.

JIM: Yeah.

RON: Right. Fair enough.

JIM: I was *introduced* as Mark's brother-in-law.

156

RON: You were introduced that way. So that's where that information came from, then. Right, okay, fair enough. Only when things are told me, they stay in my computer.

JIM: Quite so.

RON: I've got a good computer. Now, what I'm trying to say is this: We have not held up on this deal at all. Mark has held us up for a fortnight. What a lot of ballocks, for big-time men. Do you agree? A month, to do a poxy deal over a few grand!

JIM: The trouble is a breakdown in communications. You've admitted yourselves that you're batting against a sticky wicket at times, in terms of your man's attitude.

BRAD: True, true.

JIM: It's because he's not being a little flexible.

BRAD: We'll meet Friday and hope to do the deal on Monday. Your fifteen hundred quid won't be touched. If you've checked me out, Jim, you know I've got that much at least in the bank.

JIM (*pointedly*): I don't know how much taxicabs fetch on the open market these days.

(Brad barely acknowledged this further proof that Jim had checked his background. Avoiding any discussion of his position as the owner of a taxicab fleet, he went on to promise "either the photograph or the deal on Friday, but definitely the deal on Monday.")

JIM: I'll be prepared both days.

RON: Splendid, Jim. By the way, are you a police officer?

(Jim smiled and avoided the question with an attack of his own.)

JIM: We checked on your people in Miami, Ron.

RON: So what's their password?

JIM: Password? Never mind any of that.

RON: Then what about my people?

(Jim knew full well that Ron had no "people" in Miami, much less any who used passwords, but he went on with some fiction of his own, borrowed from Mark.)

JIM: If your people know anything about the power in Miami, have them ring up Frankie C.

RON: Frankie the Cuban? Mark mentioned him.

157

JIM: Have them ask Frankie about Mark.

RON: All right, I will.

JIM: Because it seems you still don't realize what Mark is all about. You don't even know who *I* am.

BRAD: Jim Cameron—that's who we thought you were.

JIM: And I told you about P.M. Associates. I've given you every opportunity to check on me. I've wanted you to.

BRAD: Well, I know that.

JIM: I was *hoping* the printer would check on Mark.

BRAD: He can check Mark out, but—

JIM: If he *had* checked, the whole deal would have been done the first day. This fifteen hundred quid would have meant nothing. The printer wouldn't have bothered asking for a token. Mark's just playing along with you blokes until you find out who he is. But you haven't even checked.

RON: Because we trust you.

BRAD: I've got the telephone number of P.M. Associates.

JIM: Which you called—

BRAD: Yes, I did.

JIM: —and I got the message you left. Now, all I'm expecting is fair play.

BRAD: I want it all to go through as planned.

RON: I *badly* want it to go through.

JIM: I'll bring thirty grand on Monday, just in case the printer wants to sell more the first time around. If the deal is on, we go straight to destination unknown and pick up the stuff, right?

BRAD: Straight down.

RON: (*to JIM*): And you can hold a shooter (*a gun*) and I'll sit next to you.

JIM: By the way, this here is only a security briefcase, just in case you think there's any hanky-panky. Quite an interesting little gadget.

BRAD: There's a lot of cute gadgets about. And devious people, too.

RON: Now, Jim, we want a little confidence off of you. How do we know you're not the Yard?

JIM: Eh?

RON: How do we know you're not the Yard?

JIM: You're the superefficient organization. You check up on that.

RON: How do we know? I'm asking you a question. Without checking up, how do we know you're not the Yard?

JIM: How do *I* know I'm not a police officer?

RON: How do *we* know you're not a police officer?

JIM: So what do you want me to say? That I'm not a police officer?

RON: Are you a police officer?

(Jim glanced out the window and saw Sergeant Franklin under a tree, his long arms raising a clipper high above his head.)

JIM: I am not a police officer.

RON: Well, that's your answer.

JIM: Ron, I want you to check up.

RON: And you're not Mark's brother-in-law, eh?

JIM: Of course I'm not his fucking brother-in-law.

RON: Okay.

JIM: I was present in the house when preliminary negotiations were taking place.

RON: Right.

JIM: And I was moving freely back and forth. If you had been as double-shrewd as we thought you might have been, you'd have had somebody watching the house.

RON (*lying*): Somebody *was* watching the house, Jim.

JIM: Mark didn't want to scare you off, so he introduced me as a brother-in-law.

RON: Yeah, I see.

JIM: Simple as that. If he'd told you the truth about the family right off, you might have been scared away.

RON: What's the truth about the family? Tell us again.

JIM: The absolute truth, Ron, is that I am part of a very large organization with worldwide contacts.

(Jim's statement was, of course, an exact description of Scotland Yard.)

RON: I see, I see.

JIM: And if you've got to ask who Frankie the Cuban is, you're in the wrong league.

RON: When I'm comfortable, I'm comfortable. And right now, I'm comfortable.

JIM: So please have your people in Miami contact Frankie C.

RON: I will.

(There was no one named Frankie the Cuban; but since Jim already knew that Ron had no underworld contacts in Miami, it wouldn't matter.)

JIM: And have them ask Frankie about Mr. *Yarry*.

RON: Who?

JIM: Mark Yarry. Y-A-double-R-Y.

RON: Y-A-double-R-Y. Mr. Yarry. Okay, that's lovely.

(Perhaps it had been impulsive for Jim to have divulged Mark's last name, but it was necessary, he felt, to "maintain the confidence level" at that moment.)

BRAD: Jim, I trust you and that's that.

RON: Me, too. I'm just very careful.

JIM: It's to your credit.

BRAD: I just don't want to go away (*to jail*). That's the only thing I don't like to think about. So I'm cautious.

JIM: I thought it would help you both if you checked on Mark. If you had done so, your man would be dealing with us in person. He'd have no hesitation.

RON: Once this goes through, it'll be so easy to do all the other business.

JIM: I suppose it will.

RON: Because there'll be no fear of you fucking us and of us fucking you. I'm not worried about nothing else. And I'll tell you what—until you parted with the money just now, we thought you was at the fuck game.

BRAD (*to RON*): Tell him the truth. (*To JIM*) We thought Mark was a copper.

JIM: Well, Mark's a very shrewd bloke.

RON: Yeah.

JIM: Never underestimate him.

RON: No, I don't.

JIM: He took the first risk when he gave you that gold bar.

RON: No, let's get it straight. *I* took the first risk by letting Dave give him the samples.

JIM: But the gold bar wasn't a bad price to pay for a few bits of paper.

RON: No, but—

JIM: In fairness, you could have run off with that gold bar.

RON: Well, now—

JIM (*laughing*): I hope this meter's not running, 'cause it's gonna cost me a bloody fortune.

RON (*laughing*): It'll come to the national debt. That's for the coffee we bought you.

JIM (*laughing with him*): At the Carlton Tower? *I* paid for the coffee.

RON (*to BRAD*): He did?

BRAD: He did.

JIM (*to RON, laughing*): You owe me a coffee.

(Ron returned to the front seat and drove out of the park again. Jim agreed to appear in front of the Park Lane Hotel on Friday morning and Brad promised to be in touch with the Magician by then, if possible.)

RON: Hold tight, Jim. I'm going to do a U-turn.

JIM: You might be able to sleep nights soon.

RON: I daren't sleep until it's really going, you know? All the time my mind's turning over. If I don't suss out someone, I'm the one that gets nicked.

BRAD: That's right, Jim. If anyone gets nicked it's us, not the Magician. He's the one who can't be caught, no matter what.

JIM: So this is a trial period. Afterward, maybe he'll get more involved.

BRAD: I suppose if you were the Old Bill, you'd be making your move right now, unless you were trying to catch the big fish.

JIM: Let me off at the Berkeley, Ron, and I'll walk back to Mark's house from there.

161

BRAD: What I'm saying, Jim, is that you *could* be the Yard and you're trying to trace the big fish.

JIM: Through you?

BRAD: I'm the bait on the hook.

JIM: Mmmm.

BRAD: So you've given me the dough and now you follow me all the way to the printer. That's the way it works, ain't it?

JIM: Maybe so.

BRAD: It's been done before, hasn't it?

JIM: I suppose.

BRAD: Well, I trust you.

JIM: If your man commits himself to this deal, we don't want him suddenly saying it's over. We want a regular business.

BRAD: I should think *he* does, too. What's better than having just one wholesaler? He says, "There it is, take it," and his worries are finished. Once he makes a printing, he destroys the plates anyway, and so it's just a shipment with no possibility of a comeback. Each lot is done with entirely new plates. Of course, he keeps the negatives. It's the negatives that count.

JIM: Yes, yes.

BRAD: See, the reason that Magician hasn't checked you out is because I'm not cracking your name to him. That's not my style.

JIM (*as they arrive at the Berkeley Hotel on Wilton Place*): I'll get out here.

RON: Okay, mate.

JIM: See you Friday.

In Brad Lewis's office safe at the taxi-fleet garage were the £1500 from Jim; in his hand was the phone, which he had answered on the first ring; and at the other end was Lee, the Magician. At last, Brad was able to use the code indicating that the payoff money had been received: "See you at the racetrack."

"All right, Brad, don't say anything else. Just pay attention."

Brad listened carefully as Lee instructed him to proceed to the Liverpool Street Station northeast of London Bridge. He was to stand next to a row of pay phones and wait until one of them rang.

After waiting nearly an hour, Brad was about to give up and leave the subway station when one of the public phones rang at last. He picked it up quickly and said hello.

"Okay, Brad—tomorrow at noon, I want you to be at Buckingham Palace. Walk back and forth alongside the wall of Grosvenor Place. I'll be driving the Rolls-Royce. Make sure to be alone. If I see anything suspicious, that's the end of it."

"I have the collateral," Brad said with enthusiasm, now that he felt able to speak freely. "The bloke parted with the money!"

"Are you being followed?"

"I don't think so."

"Be absolutely certain of it, Brad."

With that, the Magician hung up. Brad stood there for a while, having become utterly paranoid by now, and then he walked swiftly out of the subway station to his car. For the next hour or so he made every effort to determine if he was being followed. He drove round and round, through the back streets of the East End, and at one point he parked and jumped out and ran through an alley, to a second car which he'd previously left in position. Looking in his rearview mirror as he sped away, he saw no one emerge from the alley. What he failed to realize was that he had, in fact, shaken off a Scotland Yard detective who had been attempting to stay with him.

Thursday, 24 October

The Yard's plainclothes officers were keeping several individuals and locations under surveillance as part of the D.5/2 investigation. Photographic shops, printing operations, and hangouts for known counterfeit-money passers were obvious targets; but detectives were also observing Brad Lewis and Ron Schneider, maintaining surveillance on their homes and the taxicab business. Various detectives were assigned to Brad himself from time to time, without Jim Goldie's knowledge.

So Brad was being wisely cautious this morning when he picked up the £1500 from his office and stuffed the cash under his belt. From there, he took a few subway trains and then two different cabs on his way to Buckingham Palace. Arriving by noon, he began slowly walking alongside the wall on Grosvenor Place, fearful that every passing car might be driven by an undercover agent. He was reasonably certain that no one could have kept up with his movements, but the anxiety persisted.

Suddenly the Rolls-Royce passed by in the same direction in which he was walking. It seemed to slow down alongside him, but then it sped up and continued around the Palace Gardens and out of sight. Brad continued down Grosvenor Place, turned around, and started north along the wall again. When he had gone about three-quarters of the way to Hyde Park Corner and the Wellington Arch, the Rolls appeared again. It must have made a counterclockwise circle around Buckingham Palace and back down

Grosvenor Place. Now Brad was facing the car as it slowed down and, this time, stopped at the curb.

At the wheel was the white-haired gentleman whom Brad knew only as Lee. As usual, there was the confident smile and the sparkle in the eyes and the tan face in contrast to the white hair. "Hello, Brad. Why don't we go for a ride?"

Maintaining a lack of expression on his face, Brad opened the forward door and got in. Lee calmly rejoined the traffic at a normal speed and resumed his drive around the Palace grounds.

"I've got the money on me," Brad said, starting to reach for it.

"Leave it alone," Lee said. "I believe you."

Brad sat back and waited. The Magician was wearing a tan cashmere jacket with an open-collar yellow shirt and brown slacks.

"So, Brad—give me the facts on this thing. Just the facts as you know them. I don't want to hear your emotions."

"Well, sir, you should know that the American's name is Mark Yarry. He's part of a very big organization based in the States."

"That's of no concern to me, Brad. Get to the point. What, specifically, does he want from me?"

"He'll buy any amount we want to sell him."

"Oh, really? And yet he could hardly part with the payment for a thousand notes!"

"That's because he wanted a minimum of twenty thousand from the beginning."

"He still does?"

"No—he's willing to accept half that deal. A minimum of ten thousand pieces of which he already has a thousand."

"He wants nine thousand pieces next time?"

"Right. For that shipment, plus any more in the first deal, he's paying us one pound fifty per note. After that, he wants to netotiate for a lower price."

"What is your thinking about him, my friend?"

"Well, sir, I'm in favor of it. Here is one wholesaler who will take everything you can print. It eliminates the risk of us having to be involved with so many other people. It's a dream come true, I'd say."

What Brad might have added, but did not, was that it also meant the Magician would no longer have to deal with four or five other distributors. Brad could be the top man, working as the liaison between Lee and Mark.

"His minder says he'll have the balance of thirteen-five tomorrow."

"That's too soon for a transaction, though."

"I told him I'd try for Monday."

"Good, good. So meet with him tomorrow, as planned, and see if he has the cash."

"If he does, can I set the deal for Monday?"

"Well, yes. I can have nine thousand pieces for you, but the arrangement will be very special. I still think he's working for the law. Ordinarily I wouldn't make a deal anywhere near this large, as you know. But I'm intrigued. Amused, you might say."

"At what?"

"At the way the Old Bill works."

"You still think—"

"Of course, Brad. But wouldn't it be interesting if we exposed him?"

Brad wasn't sure how to reply. He certainly didn't share Lee's obvious delight over such a prospect.

"If *you* trust this Yarry," Lee went on, "and if *you* are willing to deal with him, I'll back you up. Just follow my instructions and you'll be protected as well."

By now Brad did feel that Mark and Jim were on the level. The problem, he reflected, was that it was difficult for the Magician to realize the very special nature of the situation. Mark's delay in paying the £1500 had been precisely *because* he was on the level. From the beginning, Mark had insisted on a substantially large transaction or none at all; and so his reluctance to pay for a mere one thousand forged notes was totally understandable. The fact that Mark *had* paid now removed any lingering doubt.

As the Rolls continued around Buckingham Palace, the Magician again instructed Brad to meet with "Mark's minder" tomorrow and take a look at the £13,500. Afterward, Brad should call a special number and leave a message.

"Ring up from a public phone," Lee went on. "Leave your number and I'll ring you back within an hour. If you feel sure about this deal, we'll make arrangements for the shipment on Monday."

In what seemed to be a gesture of friendship and trust, Lee went on to reveal that the special number was for an out-of-town tavern, in the south of England, operated by a relative. He also mentioned that he lived on the coast, down in Brighton. Lee then abruptly pulled to the curb. The brief meeting was over. Brad jumped out on Grosvenor Place and watched the Rolls disappear into the busy London traffic.

Friday, 25 October

Jim had been forced to wait and hope that his investment of the Yard's £1500 would not turn out to be the mistake of his life. With Mark still in the States, he felt the lack of camaraderie which had bolstered his optimism in the early stages.

Sergeant Franklin, who lived in the same neighborhood, continued to drop by and offer support; and on this morning, the Yard's prestigious Flying Squad was "unofficially" involved. For nearly six decades, the Flying Squad had taken on the burden of solving the most serious crimes faced by the Yard. Its name was connected with a variety of spectacular arrests in the past, including the apprehension of seventeen out of the nineteen persons who had gone to trial for the Great Train Robbery.

A Flying Squad officer named Sergeant Donald Warren had been assigned to assist in the D.5/2 investigation. At this moment he was parked near the pond in Hyde Park with two packages: one with the £5000 in forged currency that Jim had paid for, the other containing £13,500 in genuine bank notes from a special fund. A revolver was concealed beneath Warren's coat. Nearby, dressed in his overalls, Sergeant Franklin was pruning more trees.

Jim's goal was to lure Brad into believing that if the Magician were willing, the entire transaction would take place immediately. If it did, the Yard would have to make its move by arresting Brad and Ron. No other option was available.

"There he is," Ron Schneider said as he drove along Piccadilly toward the Park Lane Hotel. He pulled to the side and waited while Brad walked up the street to where Jim was standing. The two men greeted each other and walked to the cab. When they had climbed into the rear, Ron made one of his sudden U-turns—apparently for security reasons, although it produced the effect of making the cab dangerously conspicuous—and they were off.

"I saw the man," Brad said. "We can do everything on Monday."

"You still have my money?"

Brad nodded, indicating that Jim's £1500 were in his jacket. "The money's safe," he said.

"Look, Brad, I was all set to do the deal *today.* Right now."

"How can you?" Brad shot back angrily. "You haven't got the additional money!"

"Brad, I thought you trusted me. We had an agreement. The last time we met, I told you I'd bring that money."

"So where is it?"

Jim leaned forward. "Ron, drive to the park."

"Any special place?"

"By the pond again."

"What's going on?" Brad demanded. "What's in the park?"

"Look," Jim said, "if we're going to make a deal, you can't expect me to carry a large sum of money to an unknown destination. I mean, not all by myself. I have to look out for the firm's interests."

"So?"

"So I have to bring some protection with me."

As they rode in silence into Hyde Park, Brad thought to himself that Jim had become nervous. Apparently his "protection" was waiting in the park, with the money.

Near Broad Walk, Brad noticed a red Ford Granada parked to one side. "Stop here," Jim said. "Do you see that car?"

"What about it?"

"The money is inside. I want you to see it, because when you go back to the printer I want you to *tell* him you saw it."

"Who's the driver?"

"Brad, he doesn't know who you are. He won't even speak to you or look at you. He's there to protect the money. When we go down to get the stuff on Monday, he'll be with me. Let's go," Jim added as he opened the door on his side of the cab. "Come and take a look."

Brad stepped out of the cab and followed, but with great hesitation. From what he could see, the man behind the wheel of the red Granada was in his thirties, maybe younger, but definitely a tough-looking gangster. Probably, Brad thought, the man is armed. Glancing around, Brad also noticed a tall, powerfully built man in overalls working under a tree about forty yards away. The man was whistling to himself while collecting small branches into a pile.

Brad nervously joined Jim in the rear of the car. The man behind the wheel continued to stare straight ahead without speaking. "Close the door," Jim said. Brad did so, half-expecting to be taken for a drive. But Jim leaned forward and said to the driver, "Where's the money?"

In silence, the driver grabbed a brown briefcase from the front seat and handed it straight back, never once turning his head around. Brad watched Jim open the briefcase and saw that it was full of £5 notes.

"These are the thousand pieces we've paid for," Jim said. "I'm showing them to you to prove that Mark was telling the truth. We will *not* move this stuff until we have enough to make it worth our while. As far as Mark is concerned, and as far as the *firm* is concerned, this stuff is just going to lay there until we've done the whole deal."

"I understand," Brad said.

Jim returned the briefcase to the driver and said, "Now, where is the real stuff?" This time the man handed back a black security briefcase. Again he never turned around, obeying Jim's orders in the manner of a soldier. Jim opened the case on the rear seat and Brad stared down at stacks of £5 and £10 notes. "There it is, Brad. That's our balance of the deal. Thirteen thousand five hundred. Do you want to count it?"

Brad was impressed. He wished he were in a position to take Jim immediately to the Magician's new shipment of nine thousand notes and get it over with. The first "big" deal could be over within the next hour. He declined to count the money, adding, "I'm just sorry I don't have *my* end of it today. But we're on for Monday and that's a promise."

They left the money in the red Granada and started back to the cab, where Ron was waiting with a worried look on his face. Brad gave his associate a little nod as a sign that he had just seen the full payment.

"I'll get a lift from my man," Jim said. "And I'll see you at the Park Lane on Monday. Same time. Tell the printer the ball is in his court."

"I will," Brad said. "Look, Jim, I knew you had the money. I trust you."

He got into the front seat of the cab with Ron and they started riding out of the park. "We're on," Brad said with enthusiasm. "This time it's going to happen."

"That's what I wanted to hear," Ron said.

In the afternoon, Brad went to a public phone and rang the tavern in the south of England. A man answered and Brad asked for Lee.

"Who is speaking?"

Brad gave his name and the number of the pay phone. About twenty minutes later, it rang and he found himself talking with Lee. He told the printer that he had just seen the £13,500 with his own eyes, adding that "the Scotsman" was expecting to pay it on Monday in exchange for the £45,000 in forged notes.

"We'll have it for him," Lee said, "but I'm staying twice removed. In other words, *you* will be physically removed as well."

Lee instructed Brad to be at Buckingham Palace on

Monday morning. The forged notes would already be at a location in London. Brad would receive directions for the pickup, which he would relay to Ron by phone. The transaction would be made without either Brad or Lee having to be present.

The wider D.5/2 investigation was being carried out with the meticulous, tenacious work for which Scotland Yard was famous. Detectives were interested in a tavern in southeast England, where counterfeit-money dealers were known to hang out. Some of the £5 notes had been traced there, although no informers who frequented the place were able to come up with a single clue to the identity of the forger. Apparently the underworld was just as ignorant about the so-called Magician as the police were. Still, detectives were convinced that the tavern was somehow connected to their goal.

The next lead came from a photographic shop in London that the police had checked as a matter of routine. The shop was owned by an elderly man named Harold Peter-Lee. There was no apparent connection to the D.5/2 notes, but it turned out that Harold's son John was the operator of the suspicious tavern! Detectives had already checked on John Peter-Lee and had found no criminal record; but he did have an older brother, Sidney, who lived somewhere in or near Brighton. And, according to one informer, Sidney (nicknamed Lee) often called his brother at the tavern for messages. The detectives wanted to know why.

An investigation of Sidney Peter-Lee revealed that he was a wealthy, cultured man in his mid-forties. He drove a Rolls-Royce and frequented various dog tracks, where he displayed an uncanny ability to pick winners. The most interesting detail, however, was that "Lee" had a reputation for "disappearing" every once in a while. In fact, he was currently missing from his large house near the water.

On this Friday afternoon, without informing Jim Goldie, four detectives from the Yard journeyed south to the coastal town of Brighton. They checked into one of the resort hotels, determined to stay as long as necessary to find Sidney Peter-Lee. Before starting their search, however, the officers had a boisterous night on the town. Since it was off-season and relatively quiet, the "strange men" drew attention to themselves. By dawn, the Magician had learned of their presence.

Monday, 28 October

At Scotland Yard this morning, Jim went over the plan with his colleagues. He would show up at the Park Lane Hotel and take the members of the counterfeiting ring to Hyde Park, where Sergeant Warren of the Flying Squad would be waiting again with the £13,500. This time, Sergeant Warren would be at the wheel of a red Ford Capri. Like the Granada, it had been rented under a fictitious name and could not be traced to the Yard. As Jim had already suggested, they would get into the Capri and see the money, at which point Sergeant Warren would drive to wherever the £45,000 in forged notes had been hidden.

It was suggested that a "homing device" be placed in the Capri, so detectives in unmarked cars could stay out of sight and still be able to follow the radar bleeps; but there was no time to arrange such a sophisticated procedure. Instead, plainclothesmen on motorcycles would follow Jim's movements, each picking up the tail at various points and relaying radio instructions to the Yard, which in turn would direct the cars to the hiding place. Eleven officers on motorcycles were positioned to do the job.

At the hiding place, Jim would walk in, get a look at the forged notes, and immediately identify himself as a police officer. The back-up force of detectives would move right in, arresting Brad and Ron and anybody else in the room.

Last night Jim had spoken to Mark in New York and had told him of the plan. The reaction had been predictable: "Wait a minute, Jim! What about the Magician?"

"Under the circumstances, Mark, this is the most we can expect to accomplish."

"Does the Yard want to get the top guy or not?"

Jim groaned and explained that because he had lost possession of the £1500, the Yard was pressing hard for immediate action—even if the results fell far short of capturing the forger.

"I'm getting on a plane!" Mark shouted. "I'll be in London before noon tomorrow!"

"That's just about when the arrests should take place," Jim said.

"Can't you tell 'em to wait?"

"We've got to make the move."

"But it'll destroy all the careful work we've done! It'll blow up everything!"

Jim had gotten off the phone in a state of depression. But now, even while Mark was en route from the States, he pushed aside his frustrations and concentrated on doing the best he could.

Outside Buckingham Palace, Brad Lewis walked slowly along the pavement. If all went well, the Magician would appear and let him know the location of the forged notes. Brad would then pass the information to Ron, who would complete the transaction with Jim. He checked his watch

174

and saw that it was almost eleven. At any moment, the Rolls-Royce should be coming around the corner.

Confident that he was being backed up by plainclothesmen on eleven motorcycles and by at least ten detectives in unmarked cars, Jim stood in front of the Park Lane and waited for Ron Schneider's taxicab. Unexpectedly, Ron walked out of the hotel and greeted him.

"Where's Brad?"

"Don't worry," Ron said. "He's getting the location for us. Then he'll ring me up. Come on," he added, leading the way back into the hotel.

In the bustling lobby, they waited near a public phone where Ron said he was to receive Brad's call. The waiting went on and on, until by noon Ron was begging it to ring. When a woman went to use the phone, he stepped in front of her and declared that it was out of order. But still the call from Brad did not come.

Standing inside a coffee shop so that he could look through the window at the wall of Buckingham Palace across the street, Brad placed a collect call to the tavern in the south of England. By now the voice at the other end had become a friendly link to the forger.

"Hello?"

"It's Brad."

"Oh! I have a message for you."

"He's supposed to meet me, but he hasn't shown!"

"He's out of the country."

Brad stood there in shock as he held the phone to his ear. "He's what?"

"Out of the country. He told me to tell you he's over in Ireland."

"Ireland!"

"He has a place over there. But he can't be reached."

"He was to meet me this morning!" Brad persisted.

"Well, there were some strange men lurking around Brighton over the weekend."

"Strange men?"

"Coppers, he says. So he left the premises straight away."

Brad's stomach felt weak as he thought of how the entire deal with Jim would have to be delayed or even canceled. "When will he be back?"

"Ring here again in a couple of weeks."

"Couple of weeks!"

"It's just one of his disappearing acts. If he don't like the smell of something, he's gone."

Almost crying from anger and frustration, Brad hung up and dialed the number for the pay phone in the lobby of the Park Lane Hotel.

Jim stood several feet away while Ron took the call. The cockney seemed to be listening intently to Brad's instructions, but suddenly he stamped his foot as if in anger. Hanging up the phone, Ron looked over and gave a sideways nod of his head. Jim followed him through the hotel to the rear entrance and, outside, they got into an empty taxicab.

"Go to the park," Jim said. "We'll pick up the payment first." As Ron drove in silence, Jim dared not turn around to see if one of the motorcycle cops was behind them. He lit a cigarette, noticing that Ron was agitated, undoubtedly nervous over the upcoming transaction. "Down to the pond," Jim said. The red Capri was there, with Sergeant Warren behind the wheel. "That's my man," Jim whispered as Ron parked nearby. "Well get in the backseat and he'll show you the money. Then he'll drive us down to your location."

"Wait a minute, Jim. Hold on."

"What's the matter?"

"Jim boy, I've got some bloody bad news."

"What do you mean?"

"We've been fucked about, Jim. The printer has let us down. Brad couldn't get hold of him. We think he's across in Ireland."

"What?"

"He's got a house over there. Jim, it's a fuckin' bloody shame and I'm sorry about it."

"What's the matter with the guy? What the hell is he doing over in Ireland? What about our deal?"

"I don't know, Jim. Something scared him off. Oh, what a kick up the ballocks!"

"Ron, the man over there in that red car has thirteen thousand five hundred pounds! He got that money from the firm! It's being tied up because Mark and I trusted you!"

"Please, Jim, don't lose hope on it! Don't you think I want my cut? We've been dropped out of *all other business* from the printer because of this deal."

"So what am I supposed to tell Mark? He's back in town and I told him the deal would be done!"

"I'll ring you at P.M. Associates, okay? Soon as I know what's up."

"You do that," Jim muttered as he climbed out of the cab and slammed the door. He walked over to the red Capri and got in the front seat with Sergeant Warren. "It's off," Jim whispered. A moment later, they watched a distraught Ron Schneider drive away.

There was no police radio in the rented Capri, so it would be necessary for Jim to find a telephone and cancel the motorcycle tails and the pursuing detectives' cars. Sergeant Warren drove to 20 Wilton Place and Jim got off.

177

He rang the bell and Mark, wearing a sports shirt and gray flannel trousers and looking as dapper as ever, greeted him eagerly.

"What happened?" Mark asked as they walked inside and up to the second-floor study. "My plane got in a couple of hours ago. I called the Yard, but I couldn't get any information."

"Pour me a drink," Jim said. "A whiskey on the rocks, if you don't mind." Picking up the phone and dialing, he quickly told Mark about the morning's events, adding that the Magician was probably in Ireland. When a chief inspector came on the line, Jim said, "Goldie, here."

"Jesus Christ, where *are* you?"

"I'm at Yarry's. Why?"

"Thank God you're safe!"

"What do you mean?"

"We didn't know where you were! They lost you!"

"There was no tail on me?"

"They were expecting you to come out the front entrance of the hotel again, but—"

"At the Park Lane?"

"Yes, but you never appeared again!"

"We went out the *back* entrance" Jim said.

"Well, they couldn't find you."

Jim made his report and slowly put down the phone. He sat in the easy chair in the study, taking the drink that Mark handed him, and stared up at the ceiling.

"What's the matter?" Mark said.

"I can't believe it! I thought I was being backed up all the way! I was going to go in there and identify myself— and bam, they were going to *be* there. But I would have been all by myself! Well, maybe they're right," Jim went on, referring to his colleagues at the Yard. "The forger is calling the tune and we just don't have the power to sway him, one way or another. And anyhow, I was on my own! Eleven motorcycles, plus a small army of other cops—and they lost me!" Lacing into his scotch and becoming increasingly depressed, Jim declared bitterly that in his opinion the other detectives wanted Operation Wellington to fall flat on its face. "They want to turn around and say, 'I told you so.' I mean, I believed that whatever happened, I'd be covered. Well, shit—the only person I trust in this case from now on is you."

From Mark's vantage point, that was the best possible result of his long absence. The Yard had been unable to make any arrests, which meant that he and Jim were still unexposed. Now Jim had shifted his allegiance away from the Yard. From here on, Mark thought, *I'm directing the case. It's in my control, not the Yard's.*

"Don't worry," he said. "It'll be all right in the end."

"But what do we do now?"

"Nothing," Mark said. "It's the Magician who blew the deal this time. So we sit back and do nothing. We let Brad and Ron be the ones who feel guilty about it. Let them come back to us."

"Looks like it's over," Jim said.

"Maybe not. Keep the faith, baby."

Thursday, 31 October

Mark's trip to the States had stabilized his strained relationship with the optical company, at least for the present. All he had mentioned about the "fivers" caper was that he had been "somewhat distracted"—but he had promised to return to London with extra zeal. While he and Jim waited for further contact from Brad or Ron, he threw himself back into his job. On this morning, he left 20 Wilton Place and hailed a cab just as he had done thirty-seven days ago, when he had met up with Dave Blake. Once again he hired the cab for the day but, smiling as he spoke to the driver, made a mental note to avoid the topic of forged stamps.

Sunday,
3 November

Still no word from Brad or Ron. But this evening, Jim received a visit at home from Sergeant Franklin, who had just returned with three other detectives from Brighton. The four officers had been following up a slim lead that a man by the name of Sidney Peter-Lee (and the nickname of Lee) could be the Magician. His younger brother ran a tavern that was a known hangout for passers. And his father ran a photographic shop in London. For nine days, the detectives had searched all over Brighton and the string of resorts along the Sussex coast, including the nearby countryside and the hills called South Downs, but there had been no sign of Sidney Peter-Lee.

"There's a feeling that he might be selling notes to the IRA," Franklin said. "If anyone's got a mind to wreck the British economy, it's them. Anyhow, one of our snouts in the tavern heard he was over in Ireland."

"So is *our* man!" Jim exclaimed.

Monday,
4 November

In the dining room at 20 Wilton Place, Mark laughed at how one part of the Yard had failed to communicate with another part. If Sidney Peter-Lee was the Magician, he had been frightened away from Operation Wellington by the Yard's own detectives.

"Your own colleagues are giving you information on a need-to-know basis only," Mark said. "From now on, let's give *them* the same treatment. Don't tell 'em a damn thing unless you think they *have* to know it."

"They think I've lost the fifteen hundred pounds for sure," Jim said, shaking his head in despair.

A full week had gone by without a word from Brad or Ron. It was time, Mark felt, to make some kind of move. They would have to maneuver Brad to their side and "turn" him against the Magician. And the best tactic, Mark went on, was to reveal to Brad that they knew the Magician's identity. If they were wrong, the risk would backfire; but otherwise Brad would fully believe that the resources of "the firm" were so great that even the "elusive Pimpernel" could not escape its network of underworld spies.

"In other words," Mark said, "we've got to scare the hell out of him. Then maybe he'll get word to Mr. Peter-Lee that we mean business."

Jim picked up the phone and placed a call to Brad's office at the taxi garage. Brad came on the line and was immediately apologetic, saying that he hadn't made contact with the forger but was still trying to reach him. "It was no use in ringing you unless I got some word," he added.

"Well," Jim said, "it's time for us to meet again. Mark is back and he's angry as hell. The organization feels he's been fucked about and they're talking about retaliation. I'm trying to calm Mark down, but I could use your help."

"I see what you mean," Brad said in a worried tone of voice.

"He's so mad that he refuses to meet with you at all."

181

"He does?"

"It's understandable," Jim said. "You must agree that he has good enough reason to be annoyed."

"I've done the best I could, Jim. And I'm still hoping for it to happen."

"I tell you what, Brad. Tomorrow morning, Mark is going on a business trip to Birmingham. Why don't you come over when he's not here and we can talk things over."

"At Mark's house?"

"Yeah, but he'll be gone for the day. He's leaving very early."

"Well, okay," Brad replied in a shaky voice.

"On second thought, meet me in front of the Berkeley Hotel up the block. Just in case Mark is still at home."

By the time he had hung up, Jim was certain that Brad had been sufficiently frightened. So much for the first step of the plan.

Tuesday,
5 November

Ron Schneider showed up in front of the Berkeley and reported that Brad had thought better about making a personal appearance.

"Mark's in Birmingham," Jim said truthfully. "Why don't we go to his place for a chat?"

"You're sure he's not home?"

"Don't worry. I saw him off two hours ago."

In the study, Ron made an earnest speech: "Jim, I'd like you and Mark to make a million pounds! This hanging around and waiting is costing all of us dearly. The way I feel, fuck the printer!"

"While we're on the subject of cost," Jim said, "what's the status of my fifteen hundred pounds?"

"They're safe, Jim! Believe me—Brad has 'em under lock and key!"

"Well, I don't have to tell you that Mark is furious."

"Jim, I'm *just* as angry as Mark!"

"He's coming back this evening," Jim said, "and he'll be in no mood to go any further with this deal. But I think you and Brad might be able to help."

"How? Just let me know!"

Jim explained that Mark would arrive at London Airport, Heathrow, west of the city, at about seven-thirty. Perhaps the four of them could meet out there at the nearby Skyline Hotel.

"I can be there," Ron said, "If I can get Brad to come, I'll—"

"Well, you bring him. I'll try and persuade Mark. Then we all can sit down and see if we have a future."

"Good idea, Jim. That sounds lovely."

"The way Mark is feeling, we may not have *any* future. As a matter of fact, tell Brad to bring the fifteen hundred pounds with him. I want to make certain he hasn't fucked about with *that* part of our contract."

"When you say contract, you mean—"

"I mean the trust between those who give their word," Jim said. "In Mark's firm, it's like a family."

He stared at Ron, who nodded slowly. The implication was that the "family" was, in fact, part of organized crime. "Once you give your word," Jim went on, "that's as good as any written contract. Better, even. Do you follow what I'm saying?"

"Of course, Jim."

"So I'll see you and Brad tonight at the Skyline. Eight o'clock?"

"Eight o'clock," Ron said. "Unless we're dead, we'll be there."

Brad Lewis's frustration over being unable to reach the printer had put him into a state of extreme anxiety; and now he would have to face Mark's anger. This time, there was no doubt that things had gone wrong because of the forger's own damned cautiousness. The blame was squarely in Lee's lap, yet Brad himself was in the unenviable position of having to answer for it.

He stuffed Jim's £1500 into a paper bag and then into the pocket of his sports jacket. He would give back the cash in exchange for the £5000 worth of forged notes. He could sell the notes to one of his other buyers and walk away with at least something for his effort. But what a small return, compared to what might have been! What a disappointment, when he thought of how he might have become the Magician's sole outlet for the sale of hundreds of thousands of notes to Mark's organization.

He and Ron arrived at the Skyline Hotel at a few minutes past eight. In the lobby, Brad anxiously caught Ron by the arm and said, "I'll wait here. If it's okay, come back and tell me." Taking a seat as Ron went off to find Mark and Jim, he wondered how he had ever gotten into this situation. Wouldn't it have been better if he had concentrated on his own legitimate business? He wasn't cut out for the criminal life. All the secret phone calls and meetings, all the time and worry—it was far too much trouble.

Ron was back, standing over him. "They're at the bar by the swimming pool," he said.

"Mark is with him?"

"Yeah, he's here."

"What'd he say?"

"Nothing. He's just sitting there looking mean."

Brad took a deep breath.

The indoor swimming pool at the Skyline had a roof that could be opened up in good weather, but by now the warm season had long passed. Mark and Jim had taken a table at the edge of the pool, where they were now sipping drinks. Mark stared off sullenly as Brad and Ron shook hands with Jim and took chairs at the table. Brad, whose back was to the pool, found himself moved to make an apology. "I've been unable to reach the man at all," he said for Mark's benefit.

"I really can't believe it," Jim said. "No one is that elusive."

Brad shook his head. "He's disappeared."

"Out of the country," Ron added.

"It might take another week for me to get hold of him," Brad said. "If you want, just forget about the whole deal. It's my fault and I'm sorry."

Mark spoke up at last: "Do you want us to find him *for* you?" he said in a menacing tone.

Brad wasn't sure how to reply. At last he said, "That wouldn't be possible."

"No way," Ron echoed. "You couldn't find him in a million years, Mark. I told you—he fled the country."

"Why'd he leave?" Mark asked. "Doesn't he like the Sussex air?"

Brad looked at him. Did Mark know that the Magician lived in the south of England, on the Sussex coast?

"What do you mean?"

"He must find traveling up to London a bit difficult," Mark said coldly. "It's too bad the Brighton Belle doesn't run anymore."

Brad was so startled by the mention of Brighton that he

involuntarily sprang to his feet, knocking his chair backward toward the swimming pool. In the same motion, Brad wheeled around and lunged to try and prevent it from tipping over the edge. He grabbed it with one hand, but now, off-balance, he lost control and began to follow it toward the water. He went down on one knee and pulled it back onto the patio. It was then that he realized that his free leg had plunged in and out of the water, becoming thoroughly soaked up to the knee. In utter embarrassment, he sat down again while the other men kept a straight face.

The Brighton Belle had been a famous train, a luxurious remnant of a bygone era, traveling between Brighton and London. By referring to it, Mark had given a clear signal that he knew of the printer's home somewhere on the south coast. Forcing a smile, Brad wondered just how much more Mark knew.

Ron, who had no knowledge of the Magician's identity whatsoever, looked equally surprised. "What's that, Brad?" he inquired. "Have they sussed the printer?"

Brad was struck by the thought that once the large transaction had been about to take place, Mark's firm had sent people down to Brighton to keep watch on the Magician, whose sudden escape to Ireland was now understandable.

"Yes," he said at last. "It looks like they've sussed him." To Mark, he said: "That answers everything. It confirms the report I got that your people were resident down there." He waited for a reply, but Mark and Jim merely glanced at each other and smiled back at him. "There were some strange men lurking down in Brighton," Brad went on, "so the Magician must have gone to ground when he got word of them. Now I see they must have been *your* men."

"Well," Mark said, "who did you think they were?"

"I don't know—but the printer thought they were the police."

"Brad, they *were* my people," Mark said. "We can find anybody we want to."

"So it seems."

"We've known all along who the Magician is. Two or three *hours* after I met Ron, here, we knew everything there was to know."

Brad felt his pulse rate increasing by the second. "You knew—"

"We knew that he lived in Brighton and we knew his name."

"His name?"

"How about Sidney Peter-Lee?"

"Sidney Peter-Lee?" Brad repeated with a shaky voice. "I only know him as Lee."

"Well," Mark said with a smile, "it's quite clear that we know more about him than you do."

"Our firm's been making inquiries," Jim said. "At this point, we know more about Lee than he knows about himself."

By this time, Brad had erased any lingering doubts about Mark. If only the Magician hadn't been so bloody suspicious! "I'm glad it's in the open," he said. "The man likes to believe he can disappear without anyone finding him. He's obviously wrong."

"In this day and age," Mark said, "*nobody* can disappear."

"Okay, Mark, I'm impressed. *Now* what can we do?"

"Well," Jim said, "maybe we can figure a way to make some progress. At least all our cards are on the table."

Ron said, "I'm in favor of pushing ahead, Jim, because I trust you and Mark."

"So do I," Brad said, realizing that for the first time he meant it without qualification.

For Mark and Jim, the meeting beside the swimming pool marked a new plateau of empathy in their relationship. With only slight glances at each other, they were sharing the unspoken knowledge that their plan was working beyond all expectations. They were improvising their roles—and their dialogue, too—as if they were an experienced team. Brad had made a crucial assumption (one they hadn't anticipated) in thinking that the Yard detectives in Brighton had not been police officers but, instead, members of Mark's firm. Mark and Jim had reacted instinctively to reinforce that assumption. Now they were closer than ever to "turning" Brad to their side, making him an ally who was working for Mark instead of the Magician.

"What about our money?" Jim asked.

"It's here," Brad said. "Do you want it?"

Mark spoke up. "Look, Brad, if you don't get in touch with your man within the next week or two, the deal is off. Do you need any help in finding him?"

Brad laughed and said, "No, I'll manage."

Mark smiled back at him. "I know you will," he said. "I'm sure we'll hear from you within the next week. But please, Brad, tell the printer to stop all the nonsense. He and I should meet. For once the two top men should sit down and sort everything out."

"I agree," Brad said.

"Meanwhile," Jim persisted, "let's have the money."

Brad pulled out the bag containing the £1500 and handed it to him across the table. "What about the five grand?" he asked, referring to the forged notes. "I have another buyer for it, which would help me with expenses until we get our deal going again."

"Drop by my house at two o'clock tomorrow," Mark said. "You can pick it up then."

"Thanks," Brad replied, heartened by this further proof that Mark and Jim were not connected to the Yard. If they were, they could never return £5000 worth of forged money.

Wednesday, 6 November

Jim's superiors were delighted when he showed up in the morning with the controversial £1500. The cash was back where it belonged and the sweating was over.

"Now," Jim said, "I need the forged currency back, so I can give it to them in exchange."

"We can't let you do that," he was told. "Can you imagine if the public discovered that the Yard had allowed five thousand pounds of forged money to get into circulation?"

Jim tried to remain calm and reasonable, although beneath the surface he was in a panic. "Thy're coming for it at two o'clock," he said. "What am I supposed to tell them?"

In a private conference with Commander Grant, he explained that in order to keep things going he would have to give back either the real money or the forged notes. "One or the other," he said.

"Well, you can't return the counterfeit currency. That's out of the question."

"Then I'll need the real money back again."

"You can't do without it?"

"Absolutely not," Jim pleaded.

After several tense meetings, he found himself walking back out of the Yard's headquarters with the £1500, exactly the way he had walked in. It seemed as if he had spent the entire morning inside a revolving door.

By the time Ron showed up at Mark's house, Jim was on hand with the money. The three men sat drinking whiskey in the dining room and Mark said, "Look, Ron, here's the dough again. We want you to have it. We've thought it over and we realize that the first part of the deal is done, so here's our good faith. Now let's get on with the rest."

Ron took the money with gratitude. "Mark," he gushed, "that's just terrific. That's the way I wanted it done. This is great."

"We're not being generous," Mark said. "We just don't want you out there peddling the forgeries. I'd rather convince you that I'm telling the truth about wanting to become your only outlet. So you keep the fifteen hundred—it's yours."

Stuffing the money into a pocket, Ron was so overcome with emotion that he became drunkenly sentimental. "I hope you both make a million pounds," he rasped. "If there's any more fucking about the printer, I'll come straight back and tell you. Stand on me, boys. I won't let anyone screw you from now on." In a grand gesture of friendship, he scrawled his home telephone number on a piece of paper and slapped it down on the table. "That's how much I trust you both," he said. "Ring me at home anytime."

As Ron was about to leave, the telephone rang. Mark picked it up in the hallway, with the cockney standing next to him, and the next voice he heard was that of Sir Leslie O'Brien, the former Governor of the Bank of England, whom he had tried to reach three weeks before.

"Well, Mr. Yarry, what is the urgency?"

Mark glanced over at Ron, who could hardly conceal his

curiosity. "Well, Sir Leslie, as you know, we met at a conference sponsored by the *Institutional Investor*. And—"

"I remember. Go on."

"Well, sir, I wanted to invite you to another one."

"That's it?" came O'Brien's incredulous reply. "You told my secretary it was a matter of life and death! But it was merely to ask me about a bloody conference?"

"Yes, Sir Leslie."

"You've told me all of it?"

"Yes, Sir Leslie," Mark repeated weakly. "I'm terribly sorry, but it's a major conference, and—"

"Why don't you send me an invitation in writing?"

"Yes, I'll do that, sir," Mark said, thinking that at last he was talking to a man who would understand the importance of the counterfeiting investigation, and who had the influence to help, and yet he could not say a word about it to him because one of the middlemen was standing less than five feet away!

He hung up and turned to Ron, whose eyes seemed to beg for an explanation. "That was one of the Government officials on our payroll," Mark said. "As you'll find out, Ron, the firm has people everywhere—even at the highest levels. They're always on call to repay us with some small favor."

"Bloody fantastic," Ron whispered.

Wednesday, 13 November

There had been a drizzling rain all morning. At noon, Brad Lewis thrust his hands into the pockets of his raincoat and walked slowly up and down the sidewalk outside Buckingham Palace, waiting for the appearance of Sidney

Peter-Lee in his silver-and-gray Rolls. During the past week, Brad's entire relationship with the Magician had changed. For all practical purposes, he was now working for Mark Yarry as a member of his firm.

His loyalty had begun to shift when Lee fled to Ireland. That was bad enough, making Brad look like an absolute fool, but the disaster was compounded by the revelation that Lee had been frightened off by members of Mark's organization and not, as he had thought, by the police. It was clear that the Magician was suffering from a case of excessive paranoia. His lack of greed is admirable, Brad reflected, but he's caused us all to lose out on a windfall profit.

Brad's anger at the Magician had grown when Ron returned from Wilton Place with the £1500. It was another clear sign that Mark and Jim were on the level. Each day after that, Brad called the tavern in southeast England, only to be told that Lee was still "out of the country." On Sunday, to demonstrate his sympathy, Brad called Mark to suggest that they go out for another dinner at Mr. Chow. He, Brad, would pick up the full tab this time. He even went out and bought himself a new modern-style suit for the occasion. If he were going to move in Mark's circles, he would begin dressing accordingly.

Mark, Jim, Brad, and Ron had met at Mr. Chow's on Monday night. It was a festive dinner, with lots of joke-telling and laughter, and Brad was never so impressed by Mark's wide range of knowledge about foreign countries, gambling, horse racing, high finance, and—of course—the family. Brad was intrigued when Mark revealed that his organization wanted the Magician to print counterfeit American $20 bills.

"They realize that the reproduction of English currency is far more complicated than making a phony American bill," Mark said. "And so they figure he could turn out a masterpiece for them to use in the States. Naturally the firm would supply him with whatever he'd want. They're really looking ahead to buy into the Magician himself, to recruit his expertise on a long-term basis. But whatever happens, you two will have a place in the family in California."

At another point during the dinner, Mark announced that he was reverting to his original demand for a total of £100,000 in forged notes. "I want it all in a single lump," he said. "We've got to convince your man, because I have pressure from *my* people, you know."

"I'll try," Brad promised.

"Well, don't you think it's time the printer and I sat down, like I've been suggesting all along, and work out this deal by ourselves? Don't you agree it's gotten over your head?"

"It's true," Brad said.

"We're not accustomed to doing business on street corners," Jim said. "Or in the rain, either—much less in the backs of cabs."

"Well," Brad said, "I don't know whether the man will agree to meet with you, but I'll try to persuade him. I just hope he comes back from Ireland."

Ron delivered an emotional lecture to his partner: "It's up to you, Brad! Mark and Jim aren't going to be fucked about forever! Either the man wants the deal or he doesn't! This has been dragging on for weeks!"

Brad was furious, but sat there keeping himself under control. He said in an even tone, directing his words to Mark, "I'll do my best, but I can't promise anything. You already know what the Magician is like."

But Ron persisted, slamming his fist on the table. "Fuck the Magician!" he whispered hoarsely. "If he won't come and meet with you, I'll go kidnap the cunt myself!"

Mark and Jim burst out laughing. Ron grinned back and,

at last, Brad himself joined in the laughter. Amid the congeniality, they even joked about how the Magician had thought that Mark was an FBI agent and that Jim was the Old Bill from Scotland Yard. When someone happened to refer to a "brother-in-law," Brad made an expression of mock horror and quipped, "Let's not get into *that* again," which elicited peals of laughter from the others.

Over coffee and dessert, Ron made a toast to their success and said, "When this is over, let's all go out and celebrate!"

"Good idea," Brad agreed.

"Great," Mark joined in.

Brad took the check and created a new round of laughter by paying for it in brand-new £5 notes which, of course, looked just like the forgeries. They were genuine, but Brad moved his eyebrows up and down as if he were actually passing counterfeit money to pay for dinner.

As they were leaving the restaurant, Mark pulled Brad aside. "It's crucial that you stress to Sidney the importance of doing a large deal in one lump," he said.

Brad nodded. "It's funny," he said, "but all this time I never knew his real name."

"Brad, please ask him if he'll see me directly. Otherwise, we're going to spend another three or four weeks accomplishing absolutely nothing except spinning our wheels."

"Soon as I see him, I'll put it to him straightaway."

"The money you're spending is much more important to you, I'm sure, than the money I'm spending is to me," Mark said with an arm around Brad's shoulder. "But the *time* I'm spending is what concerns me. I don't want to waste any more of it."

"I realize," Brad said.

On the sidewalk outside Mr. Chow's that night, Mark whispered to Brad, "Tell the printer, 'Nice one, Sidney.' Okay?"

In other words, Brad should make the Magician understand that he was not quite the mystery man that he pretended to be. Mark also invited Brad to join him for lunch the following day at the Clermont Club in Berkeley Square. The entire evening was a turning point.

At half-past noon it was still drizzling—Brad's head was soaked, by now, as he continued walking alongside the Palace grounds—and, so far, there had been no sign of the Rolls-Royce. Brad's objective was to meet the Magician and lure him to the Connaught Hotel, where Mark would be waiting at one o'clock.

The plan had been made the day before, when Brad joined Mark at the posh Clermont Club for lunch. Once again he wore his new suit. He also brought some spending money, but Mark insisted on paying for everything. They wandered into the club's gambling casino, where Mark displayed an impressive ability to pick winning numbers Then Brad followed him up to the dining room for a sumptuous lunch. Just the two of them, as if they were equals. It was the first time in Brad's life that he had been inside a private club such as this one—and he could easily imagine himself spending a lot more time there in the future.

At Mark's urging, Brad went to a public phone to see if he could reach the forger. He rang up the tavern and, to his surprise, the contact said that Lee had just returned to England. After consulting with Mark, it was arranged for Brad to be paged by a waiter if a call came for him

He and Mark waited over several cups of coffee at their table. Mark said, "Look, I'm going to make a lunch reservation at the Connaught dining room for one o'clock tomorrow. I'll have Jim with me—and we'll expect you to be there with Mr. Peter-Lee."

"I'll do my best, Mark. I know it's the only way."

"He and I will sit down in a public place, where he'll have no fear of a setup, and we'll straighten out the deal once and for all."

"I'd like to be there, too, if it's okay."

"Of course, Brad. As far as I'm concerned, you and I have the same objective in mind."

"That's true, Mark."

"We're on the same team."

"That's my feeling about it," Brad said.

A waiter came by to say there was a call for Mr. Lewis. When he got to the phone, Brad identified himself and heard Lee's voice. "See you at the racetrack," Brad said, desperately using the code to signify that payoff money was available.

"I'm not sure we should continue," the Magician replied.

"But everything is set to go. It's *been* set for a couple of weeks! The collateral was all ready for us!"

"I had to leave the country. There were strange people lurking about my home. I think it was the police."

"No," Brad said, "they were Mark's people."

"What do you mean?"

"He had his own men down there. They already know who you are."

There was a long pause at the other end. At last Lee said, "Well, let's make contact."

Relieved, Brad said, "Can you make it at noon tomorrow?"

"Fine. But be sure you're alone."

Now on the following day, forty-five minutes past noon, the Rolls-Royce made its appearance. Almost blending with the fog and light rain, it came to a stop at the curb. Brad got in next to the Magician, who continued driving as he had done the first time. Everything, on the surface, was the same as before.

"Good afternoon, Brad."

Brad stared at the man whom he now knew as Sidney Peter-Lee. The forger seemed just as calm and self-confident as before. Driving slowly in the rain, with his windshield wipers rhythmically moving back and forth, he took a silver cigarette case from the pocket of his white raincoat and extended it to Brad.

"Could you light one for me? And have one yourself."

Brad lit both cigarettes, and passed one to Lee, who apologized for his untimely disappearance more than two weeks ago. He made no further mention of the "strange men" in Brighton, nor of his subsequent flight to Ireland. "What," he asked as he took back the silver case, "is the status of your relationship with Mr. Yarry?"

Brad hesitated. It was as if the Magician could read his mind. "It's on target as before," he said. "We've still got the fifteen hundred pounds, but the American considers it a down payment for a much bigger transaction. He wants to negotiate with you in person."

"What did you tell him?"

"Well, sir, he feels it's obvious that dealing with me isn't getting him anywhere."

"I apologize for that, Brad."

"He was all set with an additional thirteen-five pounds more than two weeks ago. But I couldn't deliver a shipment to him."

"Again, my apologies."

"It would have been the first of many, many transactions, I feel."

"Maybe so, but it would have been too large."

Brad tried to stifle his anger. "I thought you agreed to it," he said.

"Well, I've changed my mind. Tell Yarry he can have all the deals he wants—but only for a thousand notes at a time."

In other words, Lee had reverted to his original rule of selling no more than £5000 worth of forged notes in any single deal. Brad realized that it would be futile, if not suicidal in terms of the entire negotiations, to mention the fact that Mark had reverted to *his* original demand, which was a deal for no less than £100,000 worth of notes. Mark and the Magician were as far apart as ever.

"The point is that Yarry will no longer deal with me alone," Brad said. "He wants to sit down with you directly or else he'll forget the whole deal. In fact, he said he'd be waiting at one o'clock today, at the Connaught."

As he drove, Lee glanced over and looked at him quizzically. "He's there right now? Waiting to see me?"

"Yes, sir. I told him I'd be making contact with you and—"

"You told him I'd be there?"

"No, of course not— But I said I'd ask you, because—"

"Why all this personal contact, Brad? I mean, why doesn't he suggest the telephone?"

"I don't know, sir. He figures if he's going to spend—"

"Is he expecting *you* to be at the Connaught?"

"Yes, but only because he thinks I might bring you with me."

As he tried to coax the Magician as casually as he could, Brad grew angrier than ever. Lee was either the most cautious man in the world or the most stubborn, while Mark was equally firm about what he wanted. Brad was caught between two strong-minded, individualistic men, delivering messages back and forth from one to the other without, it seemed, any end to it.

"It's my opinion that once the two of you get together,"

198

Brad said, "then everything will go smoothly from there on."

After circling Buckingham Palace for the third time, Lee silently made a right turn at Hyde Park Corner and headed past the Dorchester Hotel in the direction of the Connaught.

In the heart of the Mayfair district north of Buckingham Palace, east of Hyde Park, the Connaught Hotel with its dark-beamed, turn-of-the-century atmosphere was a perfect setting for a confrontation between Mark Yarry and Sidney Peter-Lee. Here was the quiet luxuriousness in which two gentlemen of means could discuss their secret, illegal business without distraction.

While they waited, Mark and Jim ordered drinks at the hotel bar. For the first time during the entire course of Operation Wellington, the Yard had given Jim some expense money in order to pay for a meal. On nearly every occasion, Mark had paid for food and drink out of his own pocket, with no expectation of being reimbursed. The Yard had simply refused to believe that the American citizen could be instrumental in catching the most dangerous forger of the modern era. But now, because it seemed possible that the Magician himself was coming to lunch, Jim had been given some taxpayers' funds.

At ten minutes past one, Brad appeared in the bar. His raincoat was thoroughly drenched. Shivering from cold, he shook their hands and said, "Lee dropped me off two blocks away, in the fucking rain, and he wouldn't come with me."

Mark and Jim looked at him in disgust. "What's wrong with him?" Jim said. "Is he some kind of nut?"

"After all," Mark said, "we already know who he is. He should realize that he can't hide anymore. If we wanted to

199

go *get* him, it would take less than a few hours! All I'd have to do is make one phone call to my people!"

"I didn't want to tell him that," Brad said. "It might have scared him off for good. He's agreed to meet me again at three o'clock."

"I don't like this at all," Jim said. "We arranged to meet in this hotel because it's a public place."

"I appreciate that," Brad said, "but he's too nervous about it. You know what he's like. I screamed at him, I yelled at him, I *implored* him—just now! But there's no way he'll join us. Would a telephone call do as well?"

Mark shook his head. "Negotiate on the phone? No way!"

"Well," Jim said, "it's his loss. We can still have a nice meal."

The three men had drinks together and went into the dining room. In an Edwardian atmosphere, they ordered the most expensive lunch (courtesy of the Yard) in Brad's experience. While they sat discussing counterfeit money and the Magician's stubbornness, Jim glanced to his left and recognized Virginia Wade, the British tennis star, seated at the next table with her father, a minister. Jim smiled as he thought, If she only knew . . .

As a demonstration of his trust in them, Brad revealed the Magician's procedure of meeting him in front of Buckingham Palace in his Rolls-Royce. Then he went off, promising to try once more to bring Lee back. Mark and Jim waited over tea in the hotel lounge, but Brad returned at four o'clock with the same story. "I tried and tried to persuade him," he said, slumping into a chair, "but the man is crazy. He drove right past me in his fucking Rolls, while I'm standing in the fucking rain. At last he came around again and stopped. But he said *not* to get in, because he thought I might have been followed! Anyhow, I got him to meet me back there again at five o'clock." With a distraught look on his face, Brad added, "This is the worst day I've ever spent—aside from our lunch, that is."

Mark leaned toward him in anger. "Brad, this whole deal is *right now* going down the tube. Unless I meet with him this afternoon, that's it!"

"Brad, it's up to you," Jim echoed. "You'll have to take the initiative."

"When he picks you up," Mark said, "I'm going to be with you."

"Well." Brad sighed. "I suppose it can't hurt any. As long as everything's falling apart anyway."

The rain was still pouring when the three men entered a small café on Buckingham Palace Road. At ten minutes to five, they ordered coffee and waited until the last possible moment before venturing back outside. When they stood up to leave, Brad declared in a shaky voice that the sight of all three of them might frighten away the Magician forever.

"Jim," he said, "it's best that Mark goes with me on his own. Is that okay?"

"Well, I don't like it," Jim replied. "What if something happens? I'm Mark's bodyguard."

"It's okay," Mark said. "I'll be all right."

While Jim waited behind, Mark left the café with Brad. They hurried through the rain until they got to the entrance of Buckingham Palace, then walked back and forth, becoming thoroughly soaked. After ten minutes, Mark saw a silver-and-gray Rolls heading in their direction.

"It's him," Brad said.

Mark stood there in anticipation, but the Rolls drew near and then sped away.

"Shit!" Brad yelled at the disappearing car. To Mark he

said, "I don't think he'll pick me up if you're with me."

After five more minutes, Mark held up his hands in the rain and said, "Brad?"

"Yeah?"

"That's it, my friend! Give him my phone number if you want—but I'm not interested anymore! It's over!"

"Mark, listen, I—"

"It's been nice knowing you, Brad, but this is where it ends!"

"I'll stay behind," Brad said in desperation. "I'll wait for him!"

"You do that—I'm going home!"

Mark started across the street, the rainwater streaming down his face and neck. It was finished. The Magician was much too careful, and not nearly greedy enough, to be drawn out. Maybe, Mark thought, it was a case of a man having so much pride in his work that *real* money meant relatively little. Maybe—

Mark suddenly wheeled around and shouted, "Hey! I almost forgot!"

"Hunh?"

"Tell him we found a flaw!"

"What?" Brad yelled back.

"A flaw! Tell him his stuff has got a flaw!"

Brad held up his hands as if he could not comprehend, so Mark shrugged and turned away and continued back to the café.

Over dinner with Monica at home, Mark related how he and Jim had left the café and hailed a cab. They had gone past the front of Buckingham Palace and had seen the water-soaked, bitterly defeated figure of Brad Lewis, still pacing around in a circle in the pouring rain.

"It's over," Mark said. "I told Jim to give the Yard my

notice. I've quit the job. Maybe his superiors can call in the cavalry and arrest Brad and Ron, even Dave if they want, but I'm finished. I feel cold and wet and discouraged."

"Why?" Monica asked. "You did the best you could."

"I tried every damn ploy I could think of to get that man to meet with me—everything!"

He thought of the "selling job" he had done with Brad, first at the Skyline Hotel, then at the Mr. Chow restaurant and, continuing the following day, at the Clermont Club. Today, at the Connaught, he had really expected the Magician to show up for lunch. When that had failed, he had pushed Brad to the limit, sending him back to Buckingham Palace in the rain and then even going with him to wait for the Rolls-Royce. But it had been no use.

"I just couldn't do it," Mark went on. "Now the whole damn thing is over and I'm glad. Tomorrow I get back to work on my real job. Let the cops do what they want—I'm taking a sleeping pill and going to bed. When I wake up, I want to forget it completely."

By nine o'clock he was sleeping soundly. A little after ten, however, he felt Monica's hand on his shoulder, gently waking him. "The phone," she whispered. "It's for you."

Mark wasn't sure if it was the middle of the night or the following morning, but he reached over and picked up the extension on the night table beside the bed. He hadn't even heard it ringing.

"Hello?"

"Mark?"

"Speaking."

"Good evening. This is Lee."

ACT III

Wednesday,
13 November (continued)

He held the phone to his ear in disbelief, wondering if he had heard the voice in a dream. It had a ring of formality, of politeness and gentility, much as Mark had imagined the way the Magician's voice would sound. "Well," he said, his mind jolted to alertness, "you're one hell of a guy to try and get ahold of."

At the other end came Sidney Peter-Lee's laughter. "I realize that. You do understand my position."

"Of course. But here I'm trying to arrange a simple business discussion with you and I can't get anywhere."

"Well, I'm glad to hear an American accent."

So that was one of his concerns, Mark thought. The fact I'm not an Englishman makes it less likely that I'm an agent for Scotland Yard. "Lee," he said, "I think it would be a good idea if we could get together. We could sit down, just the two of us, and hammer out a deal."

"Why is it necessary for us to meet?"

"I don't trust the phones," Mark said.

Again, the Magician's laughter. "Neither do I."

"It would be nice for both of us to see whom we're dealing with."

"Yes."

"And we can talk this thing out."

"Okay, Mark. I'll get in touch with Brad in the morning and have him ring you. He'll arrange to pick you up to meet me."

"That's terrific, Lee. At last we're going to meet. I'm looking forward to it."

"Cheerio."

"Cheerio," Mark replied. As soon as he put down the phone, he picked it up again and dialed Jim's number at home.

"Hello?"

"Jim, it's me. You won't believe who just called."

"Who, God?"

"Better!" Mark shouted.

Thursday, 14 November

At ten o'clock in the morning, Brad called in a state of excitement to say he'd come by at three that afternoon. "Lee's agreed to meet with you!" he exclaimed.

"I know. We spoke on the phone last night."

"I'm glad, Mark. Now we can move it off center."

"Brad, I'm just curious—what changed his mind?"

"Well, he finally showed up in the rain last evening and I really gave him hell."

"Did you tell him about the firm?"

"Only in a general way, Mark. I figure it's best if you tell him yourself. But I did make it clear that you'd prefer to be his only outlet. That's something he really shouldn't turn down. It means he can eliminate his risk altogether."

"Right. Did you also tell him we found a flaw in his note?"

"Yes, I mentioned it. He was quite upset, by the way."

And just maybe, Mark thought, that one reference to the quality of his workmanship was what had made all the difference. Every appeal to the Magician's desire for profit had done nothing to lure him out of hiding. The only new element this time had been a challenge to his pride. If that were the key, it meant that Mark knew at last how to focus the mirror so that Sidney Peter-Lee would see the reflection of his dreams. The image that the Magician wanted to see was not, Mark realized, one of enormous wealth for its own sake but a vision of himself as a master forger whose work was flawless.

Jim arrived at the house shortly before noon. He had been to the Yard, where his colleagues had reacted to the news with shock and bewilderment. "You should have seen their faces," Jim said with a grin. "All I told them was, 'Yarry's meeting with the Magician this afternoon.' Their first reply was, 'Yeah, that's what you said the last time.' I said, 'Right, but the bloke called him up last night.' They couldn't believe you actually spoke to Lee. Anyhow, they're sending out a police helicopter this afternoon to keep track of your movements."

"Really?"

"They have to have surveillance, Mark. They're sitting over there wondering how they got into this situation in the first place. They're relying on you to lead their biggest counterfeiting case in history. They're totally in your hands. If something happens to you, the publicity would be a nightmare!"

And so, Mark thought, the Yard is *also* concerned mainly with image—not with the reality of my safety but with the possible repercussions in terms of public relations.

"I picked up a few details about the Magician," Jim went on.

"Fill me in," Mark said. "The more I know about the guy before I meet him, the better."

Sidney Peter-Lee was no ordinary criminal. He was patient, shrewd, and brilliant, with a grandiose plan for "breaking the Bank of England." The fact that the Yard had identified him meant very little, because he had devised a means of disappearing for weeks at a time. Detectives who were sent to follow him on a twenty-four-hour basis simply wound up scratching their heads and wondering where he had gone. Later, he would turn up in Brighton again and go about his "public" life as a wealthy, upstanding citizen.

For the Magician to be stopped, he would have to be caught in possession of his photographic negatives, from which he made his metal printing plates. The negatives, the plates, and, the Yard hoped, the machinery itself—all of it would have to be seized and confiscated. Otherwise, Peter-Lee would spend very little time, if any, in jail.

The Yard, Mark learned, had recently assigned ten additional detectives to Operation Wellington on a full-time basis. They were outside Brad's home and office, at Ron's house, in Peter-Lee's neighborhood in Brighton, at the tavern, and at the London photographic shop owned by Lee's father. There was also constant surveillance outside the house at 20 Wilton Place.

Informants at the tavern had revealed that the Magician's vow to "break the Bank of England" had become widely known. But what was his motive? Some political reason, perhaps having to do with the IRA? It was probably less complex than that. Breaking the Bank of England would be the "logical" objective of a master forger. The crisis would be positive proof, now and for the history books, that Sidney Peter-Lee was the best counterfeiter who had ever lived.

It was all a matter of ego and pride. Add a flair for mystery and romance, with a large dose of genius, and maybe it was possible to understand the Magician. From what Brad had mentioned, from what the Yard knew or conjectured, and from what he himself could imagine, Mark began to assemble a portrait of the man he was about to meet and with whom he would have to play the most delicate battle of wits in his life.

At forty-four, Sidney Peter-Lee had no recent criminal record. He had been arrested more than twenty years earlier on charges of having received and handled stolen goods. The Yard's receords showed that he had spent a few months in jail. Mark remembered Brad saying that the Magician had been perfecting his craft for more than twenty years: Ever since spending that time behind bars? Had Lee sat in his cell and dreamed of the perfect crime?

The next bit of information was that Lee was a racing-car driver. So, Mark thought, he's a man of adventure, a sportsman.

By profession, Lee was a consulting engineer. That was logical, too. Counterfeiting required a curious blend of romanticism and machines, of artistry and science. If Lee's imagination soared with visions of himself as a rugged individualist, and if he truly believed in his own omnipotence, he also had a mind for order and precision and the minutest detail. He left nothing to chance. He was an engineer who dealt with blueprints and fractions of inches.

Lee had been married nearly fifteen years. He was a family man whose house in Brighton was right on the beach, overlooking the waters of the English Channel; and there was a boathouse as well, with a yacht. He sent his three children to expensive private schools.

It was clear that over the years Lee had deliberately built up a solid structure for his life while secretly gaining the knowledge he would need as a forger. He had bided his time for two decades until he had eliminated any possibility of error.

In the past few weeks, Mark had done some reading

about the art and history of counterfeiting—as if he, too, were learning how to become a master forger. He tried to put himself into Lee's shoes, and to see through his eyes. It fascinated him, for example, to discover that counterfeiting was probably mankind's second-oldest profession. And he read with extreme interest, much as Lee must have done, about the Germans' forgery efforts during World War II.

Mark had known about the Nazis' attempt to disrupt the English economy, but not in any great detail. He read how Project Bernhard was launched during the early stages of the war and included British £5, £10, and £20 notes that were accepted without question by Swiss banks and even by the Bank of England. The phony money was used to buy carloads of British arms and to pay the salaries of German spies in England and other Allied countries. At the end of the war, the Germans loaded all their equipment and leftover bills into trucks and fled, dumping everything into an Austrian lake. Much later, nearly all the bogus notes were recovered; but some escaped the hands of the authorities and became valuable collectors' items.

For the most part, however, counterfeiting's great days were supposed to be over. There were always new attempts to flood the market, but the real "art" of forgery had thrived in the centuries before technological "progress" virtually obliterated the value of individual effort. The true forger had been a lone craftsman who used a magnifying glass and painstakingly etched his designs onto steel plates, knowing that a single error would require him to start all over again. This skilled artisan needed at least six months to prepare a suitable plate; and then, he spent weeks printing one bill at a time. His style was unique, recognized by the authorities for its own distinctive characteristics.

Sidney Peter-Lee had been born in the wrong age. He was in his mid-twenties when counterfeiting was revolutionized by photoengraving and, by the late 1950s, there was no more need for the rugged individualist. High-speed cameras, automatic engraving machines, and ultrasensitive lithographic presses replaced the steel-plate artisans. The new breed of counterfeiter was a printer who photographed a bill, attached the negatives to chemically presensitized plates, and inserted the result into a duplicator. He set a timer . . . pressed his developer button . . . and five minutes later, he was ready to run off any quantity of notes.

There had been only five or six "special" counterfeiters in Great Britain over the past two decades; but even then, in each instance, the printer's work had had some major flaw, such as a "lifeless" portrait of the Queen or a screenlike background with too much ink in it. Sometimes the letters and numbers were out of position and, usually, the colors were too dull or too bright or not even accurate. The metal "security" thread was often overlooked and never even printed; and the general "three-dimensional quality" achieved by the government, through powerful pressure on its press plates, was missing. The Magician had virtually eliminated these flaws, so that he had already taken counterfeiting to its former level as an art.

The perils of "unloading" bogus money were enough to make less ambitious men give up at the start. Most fake bills had to be tendered in dark shops, folded in half. They were quickly spotted by clerks in banks and stores, and soon there was widespread public scrutiny of bills. It meant that forgers had to sell their notes quickly and then get out of business, because their middlemen would soon be unable to obtain buyers. But the Magician's high-quality notes were creating none of those problems, allowing him all the time in the world to set up a vast distribution system. He was, in fact, creating the only "flawless" note of the new technological era while making it impossible for the police to work their way up through the labyrinth of sellers to catch him.

In 1970, Lee quietly purchased the tavern in the south of England and placed it in his younger brother's name. It was an ingenious stroke, enabling him, through his brother, to keep abreast of all the latest information and gossip from England's counterfeiting circles without ever having to associate with criminals. His brother was the proprietor of the tavern, but had no illegal connection with its patrons, making him the perfect front.

The Yard speculated that Lee had also purchased a separate house, under an assumed name, in which he had set up his printing operation. It was, no doubt, where he went when he disappeared from his family and friends in Brighton.

Mark could appreciate the complexity of what Lee had achieved. Each color of a bill required a separate printing plate. If there were five different colors or shades on one side of a bank note, it meant Lee had to create a plate for each of them. One by one, the plates had to be "run off" on the same sheet of paper, until all sections of the bill emerged. And that was just *one side* of a note.

The key factor was the creation of the negatives. Once those were perfect, the forger could destroy everything else and still have the capacity to start up again within a few days. As soon as a plate wore out, he could use the original negative to make a new one. The negatives, therefore, contained nearly all of the artistry and craft; and that, Mark realized, was why the Yard was concerned about destroying them.

To make an exact-size negative, Lee had to have a copying camera and some special film. He needed to know all about the process of color separation, too; but in places where the portraits and designs were overlapping, it was necessary for him to blow up the negative and do some intricate opaquing and retouching. The negative could then be reduced to its original size. In his developing room, Lee must have made endless numbers of contact prints to check the results.

It was no small task, however, to go on and make a set of plates worthy of the negatives. The plates were "pre-sensitized"—meaning they were coated with chemicals that responded to intense carbon lights. The negative had to be tightened against the plate with a pressure frame; and then heat passed through the transparent part of the negative. After placing the plate in a flat pan and washing it in an acid bath, the impression to be printed was all that remained.

The Yard reported that the forger was probably using a second-hand machine of European manufacture. The paper was Victory Bond, a brand name, with the correct amount of rag content. Of course, the official paper had a more rugged texture, produced under strict security conditions, and could never be duplicated exactly.

The ink was a difficult item. For each plate, the right color or shade had to be prepared through endless experimentation with various mixes. A portrait could come out too dark or too light, depending upon the ink or on how Lee adjusted the press itself. But once he got going in the right direction, with all the defects ironed out, he could turn out thousands of exact impressions in minutes.

With what satisfaction Lee must have emerged from his hiding place, having created the finest counterfeit British notes that ever existed! No wonder the forger had made the audacious move of heading straight for a large London bank and paying them directly over the counter. Had any previous forger done such a thing? By all reckoning, none would ever have taken that kind of risk. But given Sidney Peter-Lee's caution, he must have felt there was no risk at all! He went into that bank with total, unshakable confidence. He knew that he would succeed.

According to the Yard, the volume of notes pouring back to the Government had decreased by about a fifth, ever since Brad Lewis had become involved with Mark. Detectives speculated, therefore, that Brad was probably one of five men who had direct contact, in some form, with the source of the notes. Lee must have cut Brad off from further shipments until the negotiations with "the American" were resolved.

Like Brad, the other four "contacts" must have been selected with extreme care. Lee had made sure to pick men with no prior criminal records and who, because of commitments to family or business, would not be tempted to turn against him. The Magician may have revealed his true identity only to these men.

What about the house in Ireland? It was, the Yard believed, part of a plan for escape. If Lee ever had to flee from the law, he could leave all his equipment behind and take just the negatives with him. He could probably find protection within the IRA, which would be eager to set him up again as a counterfeiter—if he was not in league with the Irish terrorists already. Moreover, the Yard was convinced that Lee's yacht was not merely a pleasure craft. In the event of trouble, he could have a henchman take all the printing equipment out to sea and dump it overboard.

Mark reviewed the history: first, the £1 notes . . . now

the £5 forgeries . . . and soon, a new "tenner" being produced with secret information from a contact inside the Bank of England itself. The Magician was obviously a man committed far more to a vision of himself as some "master criminal" than to merely making a profit and quitting. If he's playing out a Walter Mitty fantasy of his own, Mark thought, I'd better keep working equally hard at mine.

Just before three o'clock, a taxicab pulled up in front of the house. From his second-floor vantage point in the drawing room, Mark saw that Brad was alone—the first time, he thought, that I've seen him actually behind the wheel of a cab.

"I'll be waiting here," Jim said. "The helicopter will keep track of you."

"Where are we going?" Mark asked as he entered the taxi.

"Kennington," Brad said, referring to a suburban section of Greater London, about half an hour away by car. As Brad drove, Mark tried to put him at ease by making small talk about California, being careful not to sound as if he were making a sales pitch. At the same time, he realized that *he* was the one who had become nervous. Was this meeting actually going to happen? Would the Magician see right through his play-acting?

When they reached Kennington Lane, Brad pulled to the side of the road and shut off the motor. "We'll wait here," he said, lighting a cigarette. Mark lit one, too, and they waited, remarking at how thick the fog had become.

Ten minutes later, the silver-and-gray Rolls came along and stopped in front of them. "That's the man," Brad said. "You go over and see if he wants me to come, too."

Mark stepped out of the cab and walked over to the Rolls. At the wheel was a handsome man with white hair and blue eyes, smoking a cigarette. He was wearing a beige overcoat.

"Good afternoon," Lee said, smiling and reaching his hand out the window to shake Mark's.

"Do you want Brad to come with us?"

"No, that won't be necessary. Tell him he can go home. When we're finished, I'll drop you off."

"Fine," Mark said, turning and heading back to the taxicab as he thought: I've met him, at last.

"Everything's cool," he told Brad. "You can take off."

Brad stared at Mark and then, as a smile spread across his face, he winked.

As Mark sat in the front of the Rolls, Lee drove off and said, "I thought we'd go back toward the center of town. We can talk on the way."

"Perfect."

"I'm sorry about this bloody English climate," Lee continued, referring to the heavy fog.

"Well," Mark said, "at heart I'm really an Anglophile. I prefer the English countryside to anyplace in the world."

Lee glanced at him. "How do I know you're an American?"

Almost as if he had been able to read Lee's mind, Mark had come prepared with his American passport. He took it out and handed it to him. Lee glanced at it quickly, then handed it back.

"How about a U.S. driver's license?" Lee said.

"Sure," Mark said, reaching for his wallet.

Lee examined it briefly. "You realize I have to be very careful."

"Of course."

"At least you're not an Englishman."

218

"I understand your concern," Mark said.

"I'm still not sure about you," Lee went on with a smile, "but the fact that you're an American makes me feel better. If you *were* English, I would just assume you were the law."

Mark laughed and said, "Boy, you are one suspicious guy. But I admire you for it. I try to be as cautious as you are, but only up to a point."

"How about a cup of tea?" Lee asked.

"Would you like to come to my house?"

"No, I prefer a public place."

"All right, Lee. How about the Berkeley Hotel? My home is just across from it."

"I go there for Sunday brunch."

"So do I," Mark said, wondering if they had ever been there at the same time. "We can go for tea or coffee and I'll walk home afterward."

"Good, Mark. I like you already."

"I'm glad."

"You shouldn't be."

"Why not?"

"Because," Lee said, smiling, "I never trust the people I like."

At 20 Wilton Place, Jim was on the phone with the Yard when he learned that the police helicopter had lost sight of Brad's taxi even before it had reached Kennington. The weather had deteriorated, forcing the chopper to turn back. Now it was four-twenty in the afternoon and the detectives had no idea of Yarry's whereabouts. Trying to avoid becoming overly concerned, Jim fixed himself a drink and settled back to wait.

Half a block away, Mark Yarry and Sidney Peter-Lee were becoming—on the surface, at least—fast friends.

They shared many of the same tastes, they discovered, and both had been startled and amused when the doorman at the Berkeley Hotel had bowed and said, "Good afternoon, Mr. Yarry. Pleased to see you, Mr. Peter-Lee."

The two men had entered the marble-floored foyer, with its pillars and fine chandeliers, and had walked into the coffee lounge off to the right. Seated in comfortable easy chairs, amid a setting reminiscent of a beautifully kept private house, they now sipped coffee in silence, appraising each other. Mark realized that Lee had yet to remove his beige overcoat. It was a sign, he thought, that the Magician was still on his guard, ready to get up and leave at any moment. The slightest wrong move, Mark thought, and this man is going to bolt.

"So," Lee said, "I assume Brad told you where I've been for the past few weeks."

It's a ploy, Mark thought. He's testing Brad's loyalty by trying to find out if he told me about the trip to Ireland.

"As far as I'm concerned, Lee, you've just been tied up on business."

Lee stared back at him. A standoff. "You know, Mark, this is one of the things I wanted to avoid."

"You mean meeting me?"

"Any potential buyer. It's against my better judgment."

"Well, it seemed the only way. We weren't getting anywhere and my people were becoming impatient."

"Your people?"

"It's a family organization."

Lee showed no reaction. "As I said before, Mark, the first problem is that I like you."

"Sorry about that." Mark laughed.

"I think you may be an agent," Lee persisted. "An American agent, employed by the Bank of England or by some other organization. You could be with the FBI or the Secret Service."

Mark looked directly into his eyes. "That's the funniest thing I ever heard."

Lee grinned. "That's exactly what the printer predicted you'd say."

Staring back at him in silence, Mark suddenly realized that Lee had referred to "the printer" as if someone *else* were the source of the notes. Is it possible? he wondered. Am I going through this routine all over again? Or is he toying with me?

Both men continued to look at each other, smiling, until they burst out laughing. "You play your part very well," Lee said.

"Thank you," Mark replied, realizing that it was essential to play it even better. "So do you," he offered.

"The printer will be pleased to hear that."

"Look," Mark said becoming angry as he forced himself more deeply into his role than ever, "I'm in this thing to make a buck. That's all I care about. You control everything, Lee. You've got all the cards, because you have what I want. I've spent weeks trying to do a deal and it's important to me that it gets done." He waited for a response, but Lee seemed content to merely listen. "I'm very impressed with your work," Mark went on, "because it's the best I've ever seen. Even if some of my people *are* a bit nervous."

"Why so?"

"Well, frankly, we have our own experts—top printers who work for us in the States. And they disagree over the quality of your product."

Lee's eyes narrowed. "In what way?"

"I don't have the technical expertise to give you a detailed answer, but it has something to do with serial numbers and color."

"Nonsense," Lee shot back. "What your people don't realize is that the British system is much more complex. The printer has studied it for years and years," he added,

221

reaching up and rubbing an earlobe. It was, Mark noticed, an unconscious gesture that seemed to be triggered when he was upset.

"Perhaps you can meet with our experts some day and straighten them out," Mark said. "I myself was quite happy that you had so many different serial numbers. I told my people there was a more than adequate 'mix' among them," he added in a display of knowledge which had come directly from Brad Lewis.

Lee's eyes brightened and he said, "The Government has an automatic numbering device. It keeps changing, so that no two bills of the same denomination are ever exactly the same, in terms of letters and numbers."

"You should have a machine like that," Mark joked.

Grinning, Lee bent forward and lowered his voice. "Do you know that the printer's original work was a *one*-pound note?"

"Tell me about it."

"It went very, very well. No problems at all. In fact, they're still turning up here and there."

"In circulation?"

"Oh, yes. The public never had any idea. It's just a trickle, now, because the printer went to ground with them. But a friend of mine picked one up the other week and offered it back to me! I told him to burn it," Lee said and laughed.

Mark laughed, too, but it occurred to him that Lee must have boasted about "the printer's" work to a "friend" or two, if only because he was so proud of what he had done. "So," Mark said, "the one-pound notes were a test?"

"So to speak, yes. The first run was paid straight into the bank, by the way."

"Is that so?"

Lee nodded. "The printer called the one-pound issue

the 'white' notes. The fivers are the 'blue' run, but right now he's working on a 'brown' run—a tenner. Soon he won't need any more distribution."

"No?"

"Well," Lee said, now beaming, "the ten-pound notes will be untraceable. He'll be able to pay them all straight into his own bank account if he likes."

"That's not realistic."

"Oh, he'll still use outlets. But within a few years he'll break the Bank of England."

"That's impossible."

Lee smiled. "Let me buy you a drink," he said.

Fearing that Mark's life was in danger, Jim Goldie had urged the Yard to continue its search for him. Now a police helicopter was up in the foggy air over the East End, and it caught sight of Brad's taxicab as it zigzagged through the narrow streets. Maybe the American was in the backseat, engaged in conversation with the forger.

The officer trying to follow the cab suddenly lost it in the fog. When the chopper moved into the clear again, there were three black cabs down below, their tops looking exactly the same. As they went off in separate directions, it was impossible to determine which one to follow. A choice was made—but a few moments later, the officer realized that this cab had the wrong license-plate number. Already the original taxi was out of sight.

It was six-thirty in the evening. Over drinks in the Berkeley lounge, Mark began to realize that he was making very little progress. It was necessary to keep assuming that Lee was the Magician, while holding up the mirror trying to focus it as sharply and precisely as possible in an effort to make him see his dreams.

"On balance," Mark was saying, "my people think your work is the greatest. What they'd *really* like to do is have you visit the States, so they'd have the opportunity to compare your techniques with theirs. They feel you might like to meet some experts on your level. Possibly you could learn some things as well."

Lee's thumb and forefinger went back up to the earlobe. "Perhaps," he said.

"Of course, they'd provide you with all the sophisticated machinery you'd need. They'd set you up in a cloistered environment, where you could produce the finest imitations in existence. You could work to your heart's content, doing what you love to do. They feel you're really not a businessman but an artist. You need protection, which they can provide."

"Right now," Lee said, "the printer's greatest problem is distribution."

"Well, my people would take care of all that. You wouldn't need to be concerned with it. Sort of the way an artist has a manager to do all the dirty work for him. You could concentrate on the quality of the printing."

Lee seemed to accept the general proposal that Mark was outlining, but avoided responding to it directly. He replied: "The only way the printer has been able to protect himself has been to do small deals, not any big ones. When you offer large parcels, you're subjecting yourself to a lot of problems."

"But—"

"He once tried to do a big deal," Lee went on, "and in the end it fell through. There was a lot of ill feeling. It made him realize that large shipments are much too risky."

In exasperation Mark said, "What are you referring to 'him' for? *You're* the printer!"

"I hear they've nicknamed him the Magician."

"Come on, Lee—cut the crap."

"As I said before, I don't trust men I feel comfortable with."

"How can I convince you to trust me?"

"It wouldn't matter, Mark. Even if you were my own brother, I wouldn't go along with what you've been asking for."

Mark rubbed his eyes. "My problem," he said, fighting to maintain some momentum, "is that I can no longer justify spending all this time without results. So you and I, right now, had better come to an agreement or forget it."

"What exactly do you want?"

"A minimum of twenty thousand pieces, or a face value of a hundred thousand pounds, for which I'm willing to pay thirty thousand pounds in cash. A straight deal. After that, if you like, you can come to the States and see our setup. My people would want to buy any negatives you create—

"Buy the negatives?"

"You'd become the firm's consultant. They'd own everything you create. In return, you'd be paid the highest salary you'd ever want. You'd have the best working conditions in the world."

"My rule is to let go of only a thousand pieces at a time."

"Look," Mark said in frustration, "that's too dangerous. We can't subject ourselves to the exposure of repeated exchanges. I'm trying to explain to you that this is a whole different league. My people are—"

"Mark, I will *not* do a big deal. What I *will* do is offer you two thousand pieces on credit. I'll guarantee at least ten transactions."

Mark lit a cigarette, thinking, After all this, the man

won't budge! "Look," he said, "I'll discuss it with my people, but I don't think they're going to go for it. How about if I come down to ten thousand pieces? That's a pretty drastic drop, to cut my demand in half."

Lee smiled. "But I've just doubled mine."

One more time, Mark thought, taking a deep breath. "Let me try and explain my position to you. Here you are, as careful a man as I've ever dealt with. I've been forced to deal with your minions for nearly two months. I've spent an enormous amount of time, and more money than you probably know, trying to do a deal. But I've failed. Also, the more complicated a deal becomes, the more turned off I am. I've never, never been placed in jeopardy, and neither have my associates. I don't want *you* placed in jeopardy, either. I simply fail to understand why we should expose ourselves to five times the risk by doing five separate transactions.

"Anyway, my people feel that you're a genius. They feel you should be concentrating on creating negatives—not even bothering to *print* the stuff. We can get people to do that kind of work, under your supervision, but we want to enable you to go on to *other* projects! You could be producing negatives for every currency in the world! That's what we want—the brilliance you can achieve in the negatives. We'd like you to start with a U.S. twenty-dollar bill, then a fifty. Or traveler's checks. We can put you in an environment where you'll have the finest equipment, the best people—and you can go about practicing your art! Why do you want to be concerned about distributing little bits of paper? It's not your talent!"

"Well," Lee said, "I'd be interested in going to the States and meeting some of your experts. But I'd still insist on doing things my way. The big deal that fell through was in Amsterdam. It cost the printer a lot of money."

"Lee, if we'd wanted to beat you out of a few pounds,

we could have run off with the thousand pieces. But what did we do? We paid you fifteen hundred pounds in cash!"

Lee smiled, and a mischievous glint came into his blue eyes. "It sure took a long time."

"Because, for all I knew," Mark hurriedly improvised, "Brad could've been trying to rip me off with a little bit of stuff that was left over from another deal! That's not my business—I don't need little shipments. I want a large transaction! Lee, please understand—this is only a very small part of what I do. I'm involved with gold and diamonds, for example. This is just a *side* deal, for me, even at a face value of a hundred grand! But," Mark went on, leaning toward him and whispering intensely, "I saw the *potential* of what can be done, because of the quality of your work! I think you're capable of producing the perfect note!"

Lee ordered another drink, then said, "Well, Mark, I'm sorry, but I'll only do ten separate ten thousand-pound transactions. That's two thousand notes at a time."

Mark slumped back in his chair. "Do you still think I'm with the law?"

The Magician hesitated. "At least you're not wired, Mark."

"How do you know that?"

"I can tell, after a while."

Despite all his frustration, Mark could not help but admire the man. He said, "You're wrong about me, but I can't fault you for having suspicions."

"At the end of the tenth transaction," Lee said, "I'd be willing to sell you the negatives for twenty-five thousand pounds. They're worth a lot more than that, but I'll make the concession if you play by my rules. Besides, the printer wants to get on with the ten-pound note and then a twenty."

Mark considered that he might have to give in, but then

he remembered that the Yard would never allow a series of small transactions, because there would be no "buy" money to cover them. They would have to arrest Brad, as middleman, but the Magician would be untouched. The only choice was to keep trying for a large deal *and* the negatives, all at once. Only then might Lee become directly involved.

"Well," Mark said, "I'll have to think about it. I'm just not prepared to accept your terms. But my people will make the final decision."

"Either way," Lee said, "I've enjoyed our conversation."

"I have too," Mark said as they stood up and shook hands.

"You still don't know who the printer is, do you?"

"I know," Mark said, realizing that Lee's main concern was to avoid being captured for the actual counterfeiting, which could mean a life sentence in prison. "In fact, I have such a strong feeling about you that I'd bet any amount on it."

"You like gambling?"

"On occasion."

"So we're *both* gamblers," Lee said, adding with a grin, "but I'm more careful."

After insisting that he pay for the drinks, Mark followed Lee into the lobby. It was seven-thirty in the evening. As they left the hotel, Mark realized that his adversary had never once taken off his beige overcoat. At the Rolls, which was parked just across the street, they shook hands again and Mark started down Wilton Place in the semi-darkness.

Having waited since three o'clock, Jim Goldie was frantic. At least two police helicopters had gone up to continue the search for Mark, but there had been no luck. Between phone calls from Superintendent Miller, who feared that "the bloody-damn Yank has wound up in the river," Jim had knocked back several scotches. He had remained upstairs in the study, refusing Monica's offer to join her and the children for dinner; and he had tried to act calm and unworried in her presence. Just before Mark walked in, Jim was ready to put out a city-wide alert for his partner and friend.

"Good God!" he cried. "Where the hell have you been?"

"Right up the street!" Mark said. "I've been in the Berkeley Hotel, having coffee and drinks with Lee!"

"Jesus! The police helicopter lost sight of you! We didn't have any idea where you were!"

In the upstairs drawing room, Mark took off his tie and lay down on the sofa, staring up at the ceiling. "I spent *four hours* with the guy," he said. "It was unbelievable, Jim—an incredible experience! There's no question that he's the Magician. But he's so damned careful—as if he *knew* I was playing a role, yet he obviously *enjoyed* himself."

Giving a blow-by blow account of his conversation with Lee, and enjoying Jim's reaction, Mark was struck by the thought that just meeting with the man had been a worthy accomplishment; but then his exhilaration waned and he moaned, "What's frustrating is that even a face-to-face confrontation with the guy means so little! It's as if *he* were playing a game with *me*, knowing he was completely safe! I'm totally wiped out, Jim, and I don't see how we're going to really catch him. The only concession he'll make is to increase the parcel to ten thousand pounds! He's just too smart. Mr. Peter-Lee let me make my whole sales pitch, but all he did was thank me for the drinks!"

"What now?"

"Jim, I'm depressed. I'm exhausted, man. He just won't do the big deal. I've tried everything. You'd better tell Tasty we're coming to an end. Unless," he added with scorn, "the Yard would like to pay for ten transactions on the chance we can get him personally involved."

Jim sat there as if he, too, were drained. He felt the letdown, the sense of failure, that Mark was experiencing; and only on second thought did he remember his professional concerns. This mysterious Yank had kept plugging at the case for seven and a half weeks, for whatever motive, only to find success just beyond his reach.

Mark was falling asleep. I'll ring him in the morning, Jim thought as he quietly left the room.

In the darkened corner of an East End pub, Brad Lewis saw the familiar figure of Sidney Peter-Lee coming toward him. Brad waited until the man he knew as the Magician had taken a seat across the table.

"Sorry I'm late," Lee said.

Brad was unable to stifle his impatience. "What happened? Did you make a deal?"

"We're too far apart. He wants ten thousand pieces. I doubled my offer to two thousand, but he doesn't think his people will accept it."

"That's all you offered?"

"I think I've been quite generous," Lee said.

Brad felt the anger rising up in his throat. He swallowed hard and said, "Don't you realize who you're dealing with?"

"I wish I knew," Lee said. "From talking to him, I've decided that he's definitely not the Yard. But it's strange, because I still don't trust him. He's not an ordinary man."

"I've been trying to tell you," Brad said, "but you just don't seem to understand!"

"What are you talking about?"

"He's the Mafia!"

It was almost one o'clock when Monica stirred beside Mark in their bed. "Someone's at the door," she whispered. He sat up in the darkness, listened, and heard someone rapping the metal knocker. Who the hell? he thought as he stumbled to the window overlooking Wilton Place. In the shadows down below, he saw Brad Lewis. What's going on? He grabbed a robe and started downstairs, wondering if the police stakeout was still on duty.

He opened the door and Brad said, "I'm sorry it's so late."

After a silence, Sidney Peter-Lee emerged from the darker shadows alongside the building. "Good evening, Mark."

"I didn't expect to see you again so soon."

"I hope we haven't disturbed your sleep."

Mark absentmindedly rubbed his forehead. "No problem," he said, "Please come in."

Shaking off his grogginess, he led the pair upstairs, quickly deciding to use the formal drawing room, which Brad had never seen. It was a way of showing respect for Lee, as if his presence called for a special setting.

The drawing room spanned the entire length of the town house, from front to back. At each end were fifteen-foot-high French-door windows, one set overlooking Wilton Place and the other leading out to a rear terrace on about the level of nearby garage rooftops. The room was every bit as impressive as the lounge in the Berkeley Hotel, with thick carpeting and a huge chandelier, and a tall mirror over the mantel of the fireplace. The most formal area of the room contained comfortable, deep sofas surrounded by an array of Regency furniture.

Seating himself, Lee acted as if he were paying a call on an old friend. He expressed admiration for the paintings, inquired about some of the antiques, and remarked that Knightsbridge was one of his favorite neighborhoods.

Mark sat back and waited, thinking, This is his move.

"I have a confession to make," Lee said at last. "Mark, I just didn't realize who you were. I didn't know you were so well organized. I'm an independent sort, so you'll have to forgive me. I didn't realize what 'family' you were talking about."

What became clear, to Mark, was that Lee had been extremely impressed by the mention of organized crime. Perhaps the forger had been flattered by the fact that he was being courted by such a powerful group.

"I thought you knew my connections," Mark said. "Obviously I assumed too much."

"I might want to make that trip to the States. It would be interesting to meet with your printers over there."

"Absolutely."

"If I went on my own, Mark, could you provide me with the proper references?"

"Of course. I would give you a personal letter. They already know your work. I'll vouch for you a hundred percent. I might even go with you."

"Splendid."

"When you're ready to go over, just let me know. I'll make some calls so they know we're coming. You'll be treated like a king."

It was apparent that Sidney Peter-Lee enjoyed this view of himself in the mirror. He was cautious by nature, but a part of him was irresistibly drawn to the fantasy.

I've got him, Mark thought. Brad was silent, but obviously pleased that the two men were enjoying each other's company.

Lee abruptly switched to a businesslike tone. "Mark, I'm willing to go along with your financial request."

"Wonderful, Lee."

"Brad will deliver ten thousand pieces sometime tomorrow."

"Fantastic," Mark said, although he realized that the Magician was still shrewdly removing himself physically from the deal. "I'm glad you changed your mind," he added. "But remember, my people are mainly interested in you—and in the negatives."

Lee smiled and said, "We can sort that out later."

"Fine," Mark said. It was best not to push him too hard. It might be possible to lead him, move by move, into checkmate; if, he thought, the Yard doesn't swoop down too soon.

"It's very late," Lee said. "I guess I should stay over in London."

"Can I offer you a guest room?" Mark quipped.

Lee grinned back. "No, thank you. I'll check into a hotel."

"Without any luggage?"

"It's no problem, Mark."

"Yes, but at one o'clock in the morning it might look suspicious. Let me book you into the Connaught. They know me there, so they won't ask any questions."

With Lee watching and listening, Mark picked up the drawing-room phone and called the Connaught Hotel. "Hello," he said, "This is Mark Yarry. I need a reservation for tonight, please. It's for a close friend of mine, . . ."

Lee made a gesture, so Mark cupped the mouthpiece with his hand. "Mr. Frazier," Lee said.

"Hello. . . . Yes, a friend. His name is Mr. Frazier. . . . Yes, he'll be checking in soon. . . . Thank you."

Lee stood and said, "I appreciate it, Mark."

"Glad to oblige."

"What time would you like Brad to make the delivery?"

"How's ten in the morning?"

"Fine, Mark."

As they were walking downstairs, Mark said, "Lee, that figure of twenty-five thousand pounds—does that still stand as far as the deal for the negatives?"

"You have my word."

"You'll throw in the printing plates as well?"

"As soon as I finish a few more runoffs."

In the stillness of Wilton Place, there was no sign of police surveillance. Somewhere, Mark thought, they must be clicking their infrared cameras at this very moment.

Friday,
15 November

When he took Mark's call at eight in the morning, Jim was ecstatic to hear that Lee had reappeared unexpectedly the night before; but he was also dismayed, because there had been no surveillance at 20 Wilton Place. "I figured everything was dead," he moaned, "so I called it off."

"Jesus," Mark exclaimed. "I wasn't worried with those guys in the house, 'cause I just figured there were cops outside! There I was, carrying on with my big act with total faith that Monica and the kids would be protected! If anything went wrong, I would've given some sort of signal, so the cavalry could come to the rescue!"

"Sorry," Jim said. "There *wasn't* any cavalry."

"*Now* you tell me," Mark said, and laughed.

"You could've handled it, old Mark."

"Thanks, buddy. Listen, guess what? Lee's ready to do

the deal! Brad's coming over at ten o'clock with fifty thousand pounds of stuff!"

"Are you serious?"

"Of course I am. I *told* you this case was a sure thing," Mark joked, reminding Jim that just several hours ago they both had given up. "So get your ass over here quick," he added.

Jim notified the Yard, being careful to suppress his excitement and insisting that the "coverage" be limited to discreet surveillance. No arrest should be made, he warned, because the objective was still to get the Magician "on the pavement." To nick only Brad Lewis would be a hollow victory.

It was two o'clock, four hours past the time when Brad had been scheduled to deliver the notes. That morning, the Yard had sent a detective to the Connaught Hotel to see if "Mr. Frazier" had spent the night there; but no one bearing that name—and no Sidney Peter Lee, either—had registered. After displaying all that camaraderie, the Magician had disappeared once more.

A few minutes later, Mark and Jim were staring out the window when Brad's taxicab pulled up. Soon he was coming through the door lugging a large, brown, soft-vinyl suitcase. Mark led the way into the dining room. In silence, Brad lifted the heavy case onto the table and began unlatching the straps on the outside. As they were loosened, the suitcase expanded from the pressure of its tightly packed contents until it had swelled like a balloon.

When Brad opened the case, Mark saw that it was crammed with forged £5 notes in transparent cellophane bags. He estimated that there were at least forty separate packages of bills. On top of the pile was a pair of plastic surgical gloves. Brad explained that the forger had instructed him to wear the gloves to avoid leaving his fingerprints on the fake money.

"There's more here than you asked for," he said. "Lee wanted you to have an excess, just in case any of the bills aren't up to standard. It's more than fifty thousand pounds. Of course, we should count it to be sure."

Mark and Jim emptied the suitcase and laid the bags side-by-side until the entire dining-room table was covered with what seemed like a large bank-robbery haul. Brad ripped open one of the cellophane packages and began to count by himself, but the bills were covered with talcum powder and slipped through the fingers of his surgical gloves. "The powder keeps the fresh notes from sticking together," Brad said as he tried again, but still the task proved too slippery. At last, he tore off the gloves and threw them back into the suitcase, muttering, "Fuck the fingerprints."

Now he counted with his bare hands. The first pile contained more than three hundred counterfeit £5 notes or a face value of £1500. The question was whether each of the other bags contained an equal amount.

"This'll take forever," Jim observed.

"I've got an idea," Mark said, quickly leaving the room. He went into the kitchen and returned with a set of scales. The idea, he explained, was to weigh the first package and then compare the others' weights. They could figure rough estimations of the amounts, which could be added up at the end. Totally absorbed, the three men went to work. Jim was in charge of the scales, taking each package from Brad and weighing it. When he called out a number, Mark jotted it down on a yellow legal pad and estimated the money value. It took just fifteen minutes to calculate that £60,000 in forged currency was spread over the table.

"Terrific!" Mark exclaimed. "Brad, this is the beginning

of a big future for you in the firm. We can look forward to great things."

"I'm glad it's working out, Mark."

"Thank God we're finally concluding this one lousy deal."

"Listen," Brad said, "I've been instructed by Lee not to accept any payment for this stuff right away. He wants you to check it over and be satisfied with the quality. If any of the notes are poor, just burn 'em."

Mark lit a cigarette and said, "How can we get the powder off?"

"Oh, that's simple enough. Do you have a spin-type clothes dryer in the house?"

"In the basement, we do. Why?"

"Just put a batch of the notes in and turn on the machine. In a few minutes the powder'll be separated. The notes'll come up to their full crispness, just like fresh money. A little heat from the dryer brings out all the color, too."

"Well done," Jim said.

"So," Brad went on, "I'll be in touch again right after the weekend. I'll ring you Monday morning. That'll give you a chance to count 'em for real and check 'em over. Then we can arrange for you to make the payment."

"How much?" Mark asked.

"Well, there's obviously more than forty-five thousand pounds in top quality here. Let's say it's a total of fifty grand or ten thousand notes. At one pound fifty per bill, you own fifteen grand."

"Fine," Mark said.

"By the way," Brad went on, "Lee would like it all in used twenty-pound notes."

When he had gone, Mark and Jim walked back inside the dining room. Without speaking, they sat down at the table and stared at the forged notes spread out in front of them.

In the basement, they dumped a stack of the notes into Monica's spin dryer and let the machine run for three minutes. Just as Brad had predicted, the bills had become fresh and crisp, with no trace of powder on them. Their full color had emerged.

While Jim began stuffing the notes back into their cellophane bags, Mark quickly put a fistful of them into his pocket. It would be nice to have some souvenirs from this caper. He could already see himself at a dinner party, holding up a £5 note and lighting a match. He envisioned the amazed expressions on all the faces when he sent the bill up in flames.

Jim walked out of the house with the heavy suitcase and hailed a cab. On the way to New Scotland Yard, he held it on his lap and thought, I mustn't get carried away. He had telephoned the Yard to give advance notice of his arrival with £60,000 worth of D.5/2 notes. Tasty Miller had shouted for joy, but Jim was thinking ahead to the next move. This was no time to bask in glory. He would have to extract £15,000 in real cash, to pay Brad and keep the case moving toward the Magician.

With special clearance, he walked straight into the Yard's basement area. Commander Grant was waiting for him, his glasses perched on the tip of his nose. Jim carried the suitcase toward him and swung it up on his desk. With Superintendent Miller and a platoon of other detectives crowding around, Jim unveiled the haul. The room exploded into cheers.

"There you are, Governor," Jim said.

Grant examined the money and said, "So what is the next step?"

"I need fifteen thousand pounds."

The commander looked up at him, frowned, and removed his glasses. "That's not possible," he said.

"Well, sir, all you have to do is take this suitcase and go right to the Bank of England. Throw it on the Governor's desk, the way I've just dropped it on yours, and tell him, 'If you don't give us fifteen thousand pounds, there's at least a million more counterfeit notes where these came from.' "

Grant's eyebrows went up.

Monday,
18 November

The decision to release £15,000 would have to be made at the highest levels of the Bank of England, whose governor was away on official business. Mark would have to stall the counterfeiters. He discussed the matter by phone with Jim, while at the same time Brad Lewis unexpectedly appeared at the front door.

"You said you'd call first," Mark told him.

"Have you checked the notes?"

"Yes, I have. Some don't have as good a quality as the rest, but I'm satisfied."

"Do you have the payment, Mark?"

"My people are gathering it together."

"In twenty-pound notes? Used bills?"

"Right, but it'll take 'em a few more days, because I have to bring in money from various sources. I don't want to just walk into a bank and withdraw fifteen grand in twenties."

When Jim arrived, the three men sat down to confer in the study. Mark mentioned that he was on his way up to Birmingham on business, although he neglected to say that it was for an appointment at an optical house.

"I'll be returning on Wednesday," he said, hoping that would give the Yard enough time to extract the Bank's £15,000. "So, Brad, you could call me at around five that afternoon. I should be back by then with the entire payment."

"Wonderful," Brad said.

Let's hope so, Mark thought.

Wednesday, 20 November

Arriving from Birmingham at noon, Mark hailed a cab at the railroad station and went directly to Knightsbridge. The forgery squad would either have clearance for the payment or the operation would be killed. Any hesitation would make both Brad and the Magician suspicious. He dialed the Yard's number and got Jim on the line.

"I'm back," Mark said.

"We've got the money."

3:15 p.m.

In the study, Jim set down a "security case" containing the £15,000 in used £20 notes. Mark was fascinated as Jim explained that the briefcase was elaborately rigged with a combination lock linked to a canister of red dye on the inside.

"If anyone tampers with this lock," Jim said, "the canister will explode. The money will be flooded with the red dye and destroyed."

"That's just brilliant," Mark said, without concealing his sarcasm. He waited while Jim carefully opened the lock with its proper combination and slowly lifted the top of the case. The money was all there, in bundles of £1000 apiece. A simple rubber band was around each stack of bills. Mark lifted one up.

"Careful!" Jim shouted. "Don't touch those notes!"

Mark dropped the packet of money in alarm. "What the hell's the matter?"

"I forgot to tell you—they're treated with a chemical. Anyone who handles these notes will have it all over his hands. It shows up under an infrared light."

Mark shook his head. "Hey, Jim, what kind of bullshit is this? Who do you think I am, James Bond?"

"It's the only way they'd release the dough."

"But now I've got this chemical stuff on my hands?"

"Yes, but—"

"Well, this is ridiculous! Especially the red-dye thing. I mean, how can Brad take the money to Lee and show it to him if he can't open the damn briefcase?"

"I don't know," Jim mumbled. "But the other options were even worse."

"What are they?"

"Well, first the Yard only wanted to give us flash money."

"Jesus! Are they crazy?"

"I told them it was out of the question. The next suggestion was that they'd give us the money only on condition that it never leaves our possession."

"That's even *more* asinine! How can we pay Brad if we aren't allowed to *give* him the damn money?"

"Aside from giving it to him inside the security case," Jim said with a look of pain, "there's only *one* way."

"What's that?"

"Well, as soon as he grabs hold of the dough, I pull out my I.D. and bust him."

Mark pounded his fist on the arm of his chair and shouted, "You mean there's no way the money can leave this house?"

"In the security case, it can."

"But when Lee opens it, the dye thing will explode!"

"Mark . . ."

"So if the Magician doesn't come here in person to get his money, he'll be untouchable!"

Jim's face was flushed. "I'm afraid so," he said.

4:30 p.m.

"Jim, we've come a long way together. To see this thing go down the tube now would be terrible. I know it could mean your career, but we've gotta let Brad take the dough out so Lee can see it."

"Mark, we can't—"

"I've got an idea. Brad believes he's now working for me. I'm going to tell him he can show the printer the money, but he's got to bring both the money and Lee back here. If he squawks, I'll explain we've got no assurance that Lee won't just take the money and run. I'll emphasize that the biggest part of the deal has yet to be done: the negatives."

"But—"

"So, Jim, let's get the money out of this dumb booby trap and put it into *my* briefcase. Please."

Jim looked at Mark with uncertainty. He walked to the bar in the study and poured himself a drink. The two men said nothing. Jim took a long swallow, as if to bolster himself, and began transferring the £20 bills to Mark's own briefcase.

5:02 p.m.

"Jim, it's Brad. Is Mark back?"

"He's here."

"Is it okay for me to come 'round?"

"We're all set. Come on over."

"Great. I'll see you."

"Cheerio," Jim said into the phone.

5:21 p.m.

Brad stood inside the study and stared down at the packets of genuine £20 notes. He had come alone. Lee had sent him in to see if he would be allowed to go free with the money. Brad lifted up a packet and began counting the bills. When he got halfway, he stopped and said, "I'm satisfied."

Mark thought, Now comes the crucial move. "Look, Brad, we still don't have our final, firm deal on the negatives and plates. We've got the fifty grand worth of notes, but the 'family' needs the negatives most of all. I want to see Lee."

Brad shifted his feet uneasily, "Why don't I deliver the money to him first? *Then* he'll come over here to see you."

"What guarantee do we have?" Jim asked.

"My word."

"Look," Mark told him, "you're *my* man now. You're responsible for the firm's money. We'll let you have it, but don't *give* it to Lee until you've brought him back here to discuss our future business. If you take it out, you're responsible to see that we don't get screwed."

"It's a question of trust," Jim put in. "We trust *you*, Brad, but we don't trust the Magician. He's run out on us before."

"I haven't let you down yet," Brad said.

"We know," Mark replied. "So we're letting you take this money to Lee. Go on, take it. But if he changes his mind about the negatives, then we'll expect you to bring the money back to us. Do you understand?"

"Yes . . ."

"Under *any* circumstances, you're to bring it back. In other words, Brad, we don't want Lee to have that money until he finishes the deal for the negatives. So take it to him, but bring him straight back here and have the dough with you."

Brad shut the briefcase and tightly gripped its handle. "I'll do my best," he said.

"We have complete faith in you," Jim told him.

"It'll take me half an hour to get to him," Brad said. "I'll ring you around six-thirty and let you know what's happening."

"Okay," Mark said, "but just remember—you're playing by *my* rules now, not his. The firm will back you up."

As Brad was leaving, Mark realized that Jim was in a state of inner turmoil. Because of me, Mark thought, he's taking a terrible risk. He made the decision, but he's scared to death and I don't blame him.

They both shook hands with Brad, who walked away with the briefcase full of money. When Mark shut the door, he looked at his friend from the Yard and said, "Well, we've made our move."

Jim winced. "And now," he said in a low voice, "we hold our breath."

5:55 p.m.

When Jim reported to the Yard that the £15,000 had left his control, he deliberately implied that it was still inside the security case, where it could not be touched without being destroyed. If the Yard knew that the money was inside Mark's briefcase instead, detectives would arrest Brad instantly.

"He's bringing the printer back here with him," Jim said, silently praying that it would turn out to be true.

"And the money?" Superintendent Miller wanted to know.

"He'll have it with him," Jim promised.

6:40 p.m.

At a location just outside central London, Brad Lewis opened Mark's briefcase and showed Sidney Peter-Lee the £15,000 in cash.

"They're expecting you back there," Brad said.

"Now?"

"Yes, because they want to discuss the negatives and, you know, the future with the firm. That's their main concern."

"Why don't you just tell them it'll take a few weeks to arrange for the negatives?"

"Because they're still suspicious," Brad said. "They think you might just take off with the dough and they'll never see you again!"

"Brad, when they gave it to you, were there any strings attached? Any conditions?"

"No," Brad lied. "Absolutely not. The only thing they said was that they wanted to discuss the future."

"So this money is ours? In other words, the transaction is complete?"

"Of course," Brad said, realizing that once again he was lying. If he revealed that Mark wanted him to bring Lee back *before* releasing the money to him, it would confirm Lee's suspicions and jeopardize everything.

"What we'll do," Lee said, "is put this money in a safe place."

Brad hesitated. "Safe place?"

"Right. Take it out of the briefcase and hide it."

"Why?" Brad asked, thinking, Now I'm caught in the middle of this. What do I do?

"If they're with the Yard," Lee went on, "it means they took a calculated risk by letting you take the money. A very shrewd move. But we'll stay just a step ahead of them."

7:10 p.m.

A technician at the Yard had come to 20 Wilton Place to install a tiny, voice-activated tape recorder in the rear of the radiator in the second-floor study. If Lee showed up, Mark was to bring him into that small room and get him to talk as much as possible. By now, however, Mark could hardly look Jim in the face. It was forty minutes past the time when Brad was to have called and he thought to himself, Yarry, you clever son of a bitch, you just outsmarted yourself. The money is gone.

7:15 p.m.

"Hello?"

"Hello, this is the operator. I have a party trying to reach you."

"Okay," Jim said into the phone. During the past three minutes, it had rung twice but the line had gone dead each time.

"Hello, Mark?"

"It's Jim."

"Can I speak to Mark?"

"Sure, hang on."

Mark took the phone. "Hello?"

"Good evening, Mark. It's Lee."

"Is everything okay?"

"Just fine."

"Lee, I'd like you to come over here so we can make our arrangements for the future."

"I can be there in an hour."

"Good. I'll be expecting you," Mark said. The question, however, was whether Brad would show up with the money.

7:24 p.m.

"The man is on his way to the house," Jim reported to the Yard. "Keep the street clear."

Every detective on the forgery squad, plus a few dozen others, had joined Operation Wellington. Nobody wanted to miss the action.

7:40 p.m.

"Knowing what we do about the Magician," Mark said, "he's totally unpredictable. If he says he'll be here in an hour, it may be three hours or never. He could be on his way to Ireland again. On the other hand, he could be standing right around the corner."

"I'm worried," Jim said. "Brad said *he* was going to ring us up. Do you think the Magician sent him away with the fifteen grand?"

"I don't know, Jim. I hope not."

The knock on the door interrupted their speculation. "What'd I tell you?" Mark said. "The guy says he'll be here in an hour and he shows up in twenty minutes!"

"Stay here," Jim said. "I'll go down."

To his relief, he found Brad at the door with Mark's briefcase in his hand. And the man with him, wearing a white raincoat, had white hair and bright blue eyes.

"Jim, this is Lee."

"At last we meet," Jim said, barely able to suppress his elation. "I was beginning to think you didn't exist."

"I won't be staying long," the Magician said. "Mark and I will probably be going over the road to the Berkeley to discuss our business."

The key was to lure Lee upstairs and make sure his words were recorded on the hidden tape machine. "Well," Jim said, "I'll just bring you up to him and the two of you can take it from there."

7:44 p.m.

Lee sat uncomfortably on the edge of the small couch, to Jim's left. Brad took a chair opposite Lee, while Mark stood to one side. There was a short silence.

Mark looked at Brad and said, "I see you've brought back my briefcase."

"Yes," Brad said. Mark reached down, lifted the case and opened it. There was nothing inside. He felt his stomach contracting into a tight knot. Jim's face had turned a sickly yellow, while Lee was suppressing a slight smile.

Jim said, "Listen, Brad, why don't you and I go down and make some coffee?"

It was, Mark knew, an attempt by Jim to get Brad alone and find out what happened to the money. Lee said, "Well, Mark, why don't you and I go to the Berkeley and conduct our business there?"

Not on your life, Mark thought. If nothing else, I'm getting you on tape.

"Lee, my wife is ill. I really wouldn't like to leave the house. The nanny has the night off and I'd be very uncomfortable leaving Monica alone with the kids. She has to go up two flights of stairs to their bedroom. I would hope at this point that you feel comfortable enough to talk to me in my own home."

Lee stood as if to leave . . . and slowly removed his raincoat.

7:58 p.m.

As he and Brad entered the kitchen, Jim whispered, "What the hell did you do with the money?"

"Lee told me to hide it in a safe place," Brad whispered back. "So I did," he added, grinning as he pulled up his shirt. Inside, tucked all the way around the waistband of his trousers, were the packets of bills.

Jim fought to stop himself from crying out with joy and giving Brad a bear hug. "The firm will be proud of you," he said.

8:12 p.m.

Now the four men were together again in the study. Mark and Lee sipped coffee and brandy, while Jim poured scotches for himself and Brad, who sat down with his drink. As he did so, the bulky money forced open the bottom button of his shirt. Mark noticed it immediately. He looked at Brad's face, trying to conceal his relief. Without a change in his own expression, Brad rebuttoned his shirt. Fortunately Lee's attention at this moment had been drawn to the bookcase next to his chair.

We've nailed him, Mark thought, and he doesn't even know it. But we still need the negatives. If only the Yard would trust us to keep going. Is there an army out there?

As they chatted, Mark and Jim went into a "good-guy–bad-guy" routine that they'd planned. Jim's task was to play the "heavy" in the conversation, allowing Mark to defend Lee as an artist whose brilliant work needed "protection" and "nurturing" by the firm.

Jim spoke first: "Lee, Mark is my boss, but I've put in a complaint to him and I think you should know about it."

"A complaint?"

"Yes. It's my feeling that a large percentage of the sixty thousand pounds we received from you is not up to standard. Some of it is plain rubbish."

"That's why I gave you an oversupply," Lee said.

"But in my estimation at least *half* is of inferior quality."

"Half?"

"Yes—and I've told Mark that I think we should renegotiate the fifteen thousand pounds."

"I'm amazed you feel that way," Lee said, rubbing his ear.

Now it was Mark's turn: "Wait a minute, Jim. That money was an investment for the future. I really don't give a damn about it. Our investment is in Lee," he said. "That's what I'm paying for. Everything is keyed around the negatives and reproducing a much larger quantity of notes. And, Lee, my people want you to work for them exclusively."

Lee smiled as if pleased by this show of appreciation for his talent. "Let me make a suggestion," he said. "Instead of you paying me twenty-five thousand pounds for the negatives, I'll give them to you free if I can work on a commission basis."

"Well," Mark said, "that would be just fine—but can I have the negatives tonight?"

The question seemed to hang in the air. Lee shook his head and replied, "No, I want to make some new ones for you. The originals have my fingerprints on them. I want to make some improvements, too. The portrait and the security thread need some reworking and touching up."

"How long will that take?"

"Two or three weeks."

If only the Yard would take the risk and wait, Mark thought, knowing that detectives were outside, ready to pounce.

Feigning ignorance, Jim asked, "By the security thread, do you mean the metal strip?"

"Right," Lee said, explaining that after the Nazis had created such high-quality counterfeit notes during World War II, the British Government introduced the paper-thin, vertical strip as a protective feature. "It's not *printed* at all," he went on. "It's an actual piece of metal inside the paper itself. The closest thing to it that the American bills have is a set of little red and blue fibers that you can barely see. The British system is better, because a magnetic-detection machine will separate any note that doesn't contain the security thread. I've photographed it, but perfect printing requires a better machine than I have. Still, I feel I can make some adjustments and achieve more consistency of precision. I'm talking about the difference of a millimeter, you understand."

"Fascinating," Jim said.

"Well," Lee replied, "it's more a matter of personal standards than any practical concern. After all, the detection machines are used *after* a bill has changed hands. The *public* would never know the security thread is missing. Only an expert could feel one of my bills and tell that the line is printed instead of real."

Mark remembered with satisfaction that this entire lecture was being recorded. He asked, "How do you make each note the proper size?"

"An electric cutter," Lee said. "I print eight bills per sheet and cut them in bulk. A child could do it."

"I doubt that," Jim said.

"Well, it *would* be easier with more sophisticated printing equipment," Lee said.

"How much would it cost?" Mark asked.

"Eight thousand pounds would cover everything."

"No problem, Lee."

"With newer machines, you can print up to six colors on both sides of the paper with only one pass through the press," Lee went on. "Of course, that's a luxury."

"But you should have it," Mark countered.

Jim exclaimed, "Lee, I've got to hand it to you. What you've accomplished is quite fine."

"It's really simple, Jim. Even *you* could do it."

"Come on." Jim laughed. "Don't be modest. If you gave me a million quid and all the tools to produce a forged five-pound note, I wouldn't know where to begin!"

They all laughed, including Brad. But Lee said, "Once you get the negatives exact, it's just a matter of having the right equipment. The machine I'm using now is twelve years old! When I get a new one, I'll print notes even better than those the Bank of England prints."

"Wait a minute," Jim said with a smile. "I know you're good, Lee, but let's be sensible about it. That brandy you're drinking must be getting to your head."

"I'm serious," Lee said, producing a pair of genuine £20 notes from his jacket. "Look here," he went on, as Mark and Jim leaned forward. "The Government itself is responsible for a number of inconsistencies. See how the color is much darker on this note than on that one? They're very, very sloppy about shading and clarity of design. With the right equipment, as I've said, I'll be able to produce undetectable forgeries that could be paid straight into any bank in the world. They'd become part of the currency without the Government knowing it before it's too late. It would break the Bank of England for sure."

"Amazing," Mark said.

"What I'm planning is to print the notes *outside* this country. That way, there'd be no risk of being discovered at the source by Scotland Yard. The press and facilities would be completely safe."

"Where?" Mark asked.

Lee hesitated, then replied, "Ireland. The notes would come back to England by that route." In the silence, as he refilled the brandy glasses, Mark wondered whether to press him about any involvement with the IRA, but he was afraid to raise more suspicion than already existed. "By the way," Lee said with enthusiasm, "let me point out something to you both." He took a genuine £5 note from his pocket and asked for a forgery with which to compare it. Eager to help him further incriminate himself, Mark retrieved one of his "souvenirs" from the desk and handed it to him.

Lee spread the two notes on the coffee table and announced that there was a "code system" for the serial numbers. He pointed to the lower-left corner of the back of his genuine fiver, indicating a tiny, almost-imperceptible "L" that had been printed just to the right of the £5 sign.

"Now," Lee said, as if instructing a class of counterfeiting students, "that small letter is a secret code used by the Bank of England. It's quite simple, but most people don't even notice, for instance, that if the code is there, then the numbers precede the letter on the face of the note. If there *isn't* any 'L' in back, then the letter will precede the numbers."

"I never realized that," Jim said truthfully.

"*This* genuine bill, for example, has the tiny code on the back," Lee said. He flipped it over and pointed to the face of the note, adding, "So the number here is sixty-four D. If the 'L' was missing, it would be D sixty-four. And here's *my* note—which, you can see, has it matched up correctly."

"Marvelous," Mark said.

"No, no, it's just a small point," Lee replied as he leaned back. At Mark's urging, he reiterated how successful his earlier £1 notes had been, then repeated—unwittingly, again, for the tape machine—his intention to produce large runs of £10 notes to coincide with the Bank of England's still-secret issuance. "The Government's note will be on the street before Christmas," he said, "and *my* note will be ready at the same time."

"Fantastic," Mark said. "That's another stroke of genius on your part."

Suddenly a clicking sound came from the radiator and the men fell silent. At the noise continued, Mark realized that the concealed tape recorder had somehow gone out of control.

Lee glanced over and said, "What's that?"

"The central heating," Mark found himself saying. "It just went on."

The Magician stared at Mark and said, "I have a sixth sense about some things. I like you, as I've mentioned. You're very smooth, Mark. And yet I keep having the notion that you're a CIA agent on loan to the Bank of England."

"He *is*," Jim said with a smile. "And I'm a Metropolitan Police officer."

Brad squirmed and got to his feet. "Don't let's start that again," he moaned.

"You could be," Lee pressed. "You're tall enough, Jim, and you've got that curly hair that detectives have."

Jim stared back until Lee smiled, but Brad refused to acknowledge any humor in this conversation. Jim said his bladder was full and excused himself.

254

10:25 p.m.

He went into the bathroom, pressed down the flusher and slipped out again. He quietly proceeded to the third-floor master bedroom. As instructed, Monica was on the top floor with the children. Jim picked up the phone and dialed a special number for the Yard's radio dispatcher.

"They'll be coming out soon," he said in a low voice. "They're in possession of the money. I'll ring back."

He gently replaced the phone and started downstairs. Below, on the second-floor landing, Brad Lewis was staring up at him.

"Where were you?"

"Upstairs," Jim said. "Checking on the kids."

10:40 p.m.

"Lee, I'd really like you to take that trip with me to the States," Mark was saying. "Your passport's up-to-date, isn't it?"

"Of course."

"I want to show you the setup there," Mark went on, "I still believe that you deserve special conditions so you can do your best work. You could eventually bring over your family and settle there. You'd be happy and insulated and safe. Treated like royalty. And if you prefer, it *could* be on a commission basis, the way you suggested."

Was the Magician looking at the ideal image of himself? Given the time, Mark thought, I could lure him even further into that fantasy world; and if the Yard would wait just two or three more weeks, I'm sure he'd return with his new set of negatives, in full faith that the illusion is real.

10:43 p.m.

With Brad to one side, Mark and Lee stood facing each other at the door. Lee promised to be in touch within the next few days, to make plans for his initial trip to the States. Was he still just toying with the whole idea? Or was he drawn irresistibly, as Mark had been, deeper and deeper into his role? It starts with a notion, becomes a fantasy, transforms itself into fierce desire, then into the action itself . . .

Yes, Mark thought, the Magician is ready to hop a plane, to take flight, to see where it brings him. He and I are more alike than we know.

As they shook hands, however, Mark realized that Lee was still gazing at him and trying to discover the truth.

10:44 p.m.

Alone in the study, Jim said into the phone, "They're on their way. Give the word in thirty seconds." As planned, the radio dispatcher would call out, "Wellington! Wellington!"—the signal for detectives hiding all over Wilton Place to make their move.

10:45 p.m.

"Cheerio," Mark said as he waved to the forger and shut the door. He turned and raced upstairs to the drawing room, where he and Jim could look out the window at the scene on Wilton Place. Lee and Brad were just emerging onto the patio in the darkness, heading for the street. Jim switched on a special police radio so they could hear the communications between headquarters and the field. Any moment now, the "Wellington" signal was coming. The dozens of cops would respond by jumping out of their hiding places.

"We didn't get the negatives," Mark said. "Do they *have* to make the bust?"

"They do," Jim said. "We can't let the money go out."

I've trapped him, Mark thought, but only as a seller of counterfeit money, not as the forger. We've both won the game. He had the sudden urge to lean out the window and warn his adversary, to tell him how much he admired him as a man of imagination and adventure—and, in a deeper way, to express his own affection and feelings of kinship toward him. In the next few seconds, Britain's most brilliant counterfeiter was about to be captured and hauled away like a common criminal, yet there was nothing common, and certainly nothing murderous or violent, about Sidney Peter-Lee. Why, Mark thought, does the Walter Mitty play have to come to an end? Why can't they bring the curtain down so the actors can all go home? Why does it have to affect our real lives?

Down below, Lee and Brad were stepping off the curb.

"Waterloo!" came the radio dispatcher's voice. "Waterloo!"

Mark and Jim looked at each other. It was the wrong signal. Sidney Peter-Lee and Brad Lewis were starting across the street, but nothing was happening! They were going free!

"Waterloo! Waterloo!"

Is it possible, Mark thought, that yet another miraculous fuck-up is taking place? Will they let the Magician get away, so he can come back another time with the negatives? He's still walking . . .

"Oh, shit!" came the dispatcher's voice. "Wellington! Wellington!"

10:47 p.m.

In the middle of the street, Lee walked slowly with Brad beside him. It was so dark, so still, and so quiet that when the first shadow began to move he suddenly stopped. He stood listening and trying to focus his eyes. Something made him glance over his shoulder and upward, to the second-floor window of 20 Wilton Place. Mark's face, and Mark's eyes, were staring down at him. For just a second, Lee saw the reflection of his dreams in the mirror; but then the reality of the face was clear, the reality that he had known from the beginning. At this moment of defeat, even without understanding the exact nature of his checkmated position, he turned again toward the darkness. Now all the shadows were moving. The Magician waited calmly, with the dignity of a man always in complete control.

Epilogue

Mark and Jim gazed down at the scene below the drawing-room window as officers of the law sprang forth to make the arrest. For Mark, it meant the complete shattering of the fantasy that he had built up during the past nine weeks, as if he were suddenly awakening from a long, vivid daydream.

When the cops burst out of the shadows, Brad Lewis started to run. After all, he was carrying £15,000 in cash; and his first impression was that he was about to become the victim of a robbery. He fled toward his taxicab, but then came the realization that his attackers were, in fact, detectives. In panic and bewilderment, he found himself swept off his feet and thrown atop the hood of the cab. He was slammed down on his back, and pinned, while his shirt was ripped open and the money recovered.

Sidney Peter-Lee remained standing in the street as if to say, "Well, gentlemen, what can I do for you?" From this moment on, he would be one of the most gracious—and evasive—prisoners in memory.

While these arrests were in progress, Dave Blake was picked up at home and brought in for questioning; and Sergeant Franklin knocked at the door of Ron Schneider's house. When the cockney answered, he began to protest: "Forged fivers? You've got to be joking! There's nothing here like that! You can see for yourself!" Franklin searched the house, but found nothing. Ron pleaded, "I'm in the dark about all this!"

" 'Tis of wee consequence," Franklin replied. "You are under arrest for being involved with forged currency."

"But I'm just a tiny cog in a big wheel!" Ron protested as Franklin, who seemed twice his size, lifted him up and pointed him toward the door.

In their separate cells and interrogation rooms, the prisoners at first refused to speak. Eventually statements were made by Brad, Ron, and Dave—but the Magician kept silent.

Still convinced that Mark was part of an organized-crime syndicate, Ron told the officers, "There's more involved here than you realize. It's bigger than all of us! I've got bloody good reason to be scared," he went on, apparently without the slightest suspicion that Mark and Jim had been posing.

Brad Lewis admitted almost everything, yet he steadfastly protected both the American and the forger. He refused to reveal Mark's last name and avoided any mention of "the firm," while also hinting that Lee was not, after all, the forger.

"Mr. Peter-Lee was very secretive about where he got the forged five-pound notes," Brad told the police. "As far as I'm concerned, I asked him for the notes and he produced them."

Superintendent Miller interviewed Lee, stressing that the Yard was mainly concerned about the printing plates and photographic negatives.

"I would like to see someone from the Bank of England," Lee replied. "It would be to their advantage."

"Well . . ."

"I can help them," Lee offered.

"Will you make a statement?"

"No, but I'd like to show the Bank how it could tighten up its security system."

With mind-boggling stuffiness, the Government would not arrange such a meeting between the Bank of England and the man who had been duplicating its notes so authentically.

At one point, Lee was paid a visit by another detective from the forgery squad. The Magician made a little bow in greeting and said, "I wish to thank you, and all the officers, for the kind way these inquiries have been conducted." Then, intrigued that the detective dealt with counterfeit currency, he added, "It must be interesting for you, working with bank notes and coins."

"Well, yes, it is."

"There have been some excellent forgeries in the past several years," Lee continued. "I suppose the Swiss franc was one of the best, eh?"

"I believe so," the detective replied.

"But the five-pound note is just as good, don't you think?" Lee asked, referring to his own work.

"Maybe better."

Lee's face brightened. "How much do you think the entire job cost?"

"Six thousand pounds?"

The Magician laughed. "*One* thousand," he exclaimed. "It was all done on an old machine."

"It's certainly a very good note."

"Well," Lee said eagerly, "I would be extremely interested to see the Yard's forgery collection. . . ."

Dave, Ron, and Brad were released on bail, in that order. A much higher bail was set for Lee, who preferred to stay in prison. Apparently reasoning that he was destined to serve time in any event, he elected to remain in jail and have the pretrial waiting period credited toward his eventual sentence.

On Christmas Eve, Mark Yarry received word from the optical company that his employment had been terminated. Even though his sales had begun to climb in recent weeks, it was felt that his mind had never really been on the job.

Meanwhile, all the officers who had been involved in the D.5/2 case were being promoted. Jim Goldie was on his way to becoming a sergeant and was transferred to the prestigious Flying Squad.

The forger's machinery was never found. The plates and negatives may or may not have been destroyed, but they, too, were never recovered. Moreoever, the Yard's tape recorder, positioned secretly in the second-floor study of 20 Wilton Place, had failed to pick up Sidney Peter-Lee's discussion of his role in printing the notes. All that could be heard on the tape was a steady hum, further confirming the aptness of Lee's reputation as the Magician.

In the first few months of 1975 the Yard received information that Lee had been in contact with the IRA, but no proof could be obtained. No evidence of any sort was found at his house in southern Ireland.

The trial for those arrested in "The Great Fivers Plot" was scheduled for mid-June. Prosecutor Henry Pownall made plans to rearrange his busy schedule so he could personally handle the case. Also, some of the most prestigious lawyers in London offered their services to the defenders. But just before the trial was to begin, the Government offered to play some of Jim Goldie's secret tape recordings of his meetings with Brad and Ron. What the attorneys heard was so devastating that they advised their clients to plead guilty to a charge of conspiring to utter forged notes.

Lee, too, elected to plead guilty, so that within the courtroom the forger's identity would remain a mystery. Although Lee had been arrested with an associate (Brad) who was in possession of payoff money, there would be no way to prove that he had printed the fivers—even though the number of notes in circulation had dwindled to virtually zero, and no forged "tenners" ever appeared.

The hearings at the Old Bailey took place on the eighteenth and nineteenth of June 1975. Amid the pure-theater spectacle of black gowns and white wigs, the scarlet-robed judge, King-Hamilton, gave Dave Blake a suspended sentence while sending Ron Schneider to prison for eighteen months and putting Brad Lewis away for four years. Sidney Peter-Lee remained in the dock.

"Forging and uttering bank notes is always regarded as a very serious matter," the judge told him, "and Parliament has laid down, as you probably know, that the maximum penalty is imprisonment for life. One witness even said that you, Peter-Lee, expressed the intention to 'break the Bank of England.' Well, I do not know, of course, if you said it, and I don't even know, if you did say it, whether it was said seriously or in jest. But, you know, taken to its logical conclusion, putting countless thousands of forged five-pound notes into circulation would tend to do ultimately just that."

For lack of evidence, Lee escaped a lifetime sentence and, instead, was given five years. In 1980 an official of the Yard declared that the case had "put an end to all forgeries in England" because it had frightened off any potential counterfeiters.

"It is obvious," the judge said, "that when Mr. Yarry realized what was happening he got in touch with his own embassy to seek advice, and as a result of that advice he went to Scotland Yard and then cooperated wholly with the police, in the most spirited way, acting on their instructions and playing the role assigned to him quite magnificently, so it seems, and the authorities have reason to be grateful to him. As I believe he is present in court, he will have heard me make this commendation.

"With regard to Detective Constable Goldie, a young CID officer, he exercised enormous skill and courage; indeed, courage of a very high order. He was not to know what might happen to him at any time if any of those with him should suddenly turn violent on realizing that he was a police officer, as they so nearly did, and even in those moments when they so nearly discovered it he did not weaken and disclose it. And his conduct deserves, in my judgment, the highest commendation, because he behaved in a manner in keeping with the great tradition of the CID and the police force in this country.

"Had I got it in my power, which I have not, to award these two gentlemen an Oscar, I would do it."

The play was over. The Magician left the stage for a prison cell, his identity as the forger still beyond the reach of the law. The American departed from England to seek another role.

Sources

Witness Statements of James Goldie and Mark Yarry.
Statements given to police by Brad Lewis, Ron Schneider, and Dave Blake.
Transcript of Old Bailey court proceedings.
Personal notes and diaries of Mark Yarry.
Interviews with Mark Yarry.
Interviews with James Goldie.
Interview with Sergeant Edward Franklin.
Interview with Brad Lewis.
Pretrial notes taken by the Government Prosecutor.
Statement from the Bank of England Printing Works.
Transcripts of Goldie's tape recordings of various meetings, including several in Hyde Park and one in Mr. Chow restaurant.
Other interviews, off-the-record.